Working Juju

Working Juju

REPRESENTATIONS OF THE CARIBBEAN FANTASTIC

Andrea Shaw Nevins

THE UNIVERSITY OF GEORGIA PRESS
ATHENS

Paperback edition, 2023
© 2019 by the University of Georgia Press
Athens, Georgia 30602
www.ugapress.org
All rights reserved
Designed by Kaelin Chappell Broaddus
Set in 11.5/14 Fournier MT Std by Kaelin Chappell Broaddus

Most University of Georgia Press titles are
available from popular e-book vendors.

Printed digitally

The Library of Congress has catalogued the
hardcover edition of this book as follows:

NAMES: Shaw Nevins, Andrea, 1965– author.
TITLE: Working juju : representations of the Caribbean fantastic / Andrea Shaw Nevins.
DESCRIPTION: Athens : The University of Georgia Press, 2019. | Includes bibliographical references and index.
IDENTIFIERS: LCCN 2019018154 | ISBN 9780820356099 (hardback : alk. paper) | ISBN 9780820356105 (ebook)
SUBJECTS: LCSH: Caribbean literature (English)—History and criticism. | Fantastic, The, in literature. | Fantastic, The, in art. | Magic in literature. | Caribbean Area—Civilization. | Caribbean Area—Social life and customs. | Religion and literature—Caribbean Area—History. | Literature and society—Caribbean Area—History. | Literature and history—Caribbean Area—History. | Caribbean Area—Intellectual life.
CLASSIFICATION: LCC PR9205 .S53 2019 | DDC 810.9/9729—dc23
LC record available at https://lccn.loc.gov/2019018154

Paperback ISBN 978-0-8203-6615-9

For my mother,
Mrs. Kathleen "Iris" Shaw,
whose love has taken me to the
most fantastic of places.

CONTENTS

ACKNOWLEDGMENTS
ix

INTRODUCTION
Kingdoms in Other Worlds
The Science of Working Juju
1

CHAPTER 1
British Obeah
The Making of Caribbean Savages
26

CHAPTER 2
Devilish Divas and Gangster Monsters
Hollywood's Monstrous Imaginings of the Caribbean
42

CHAPTER 3
The Haunting of a Nation
Death and Discourse in Jamaica
78

CHAPTER 4
Exodus
*The Intergalactic Movement of Jah People
in the Works of Tobias Buckell*
100

CONCLUSION
Seeing Strange Things
Fantastical Visual Portrayals of the Caribbean
125

APPENDIX
Interview with Tobias Buckell
135

NOTES
145

INDEX
163

ACKNOWLEDGMENTS

My sincerest appreciation to all the friends and family whose passionate support of anything I pursue has helped me have any success worth mentioning. Thanks to my colleagues at Nova Southeastern University and elsewhere for your encouragement and suggestions. I would especially like to acknowledge the feedback from the anonymous reviewers selected by University of Georgia Press. Their comments were exceedingly thoughtful and detailed, and they have helped me write a better book. Special thanks to Don Rosenblum and Marlisa Santos for supporting my requests for course releases and mini-grants in the earliest stages of this project. Thanks to Honggang Yang, who enabled me to have the support of graduate assistants as the project progressed—this help was invaluable. Those student assistants include Kimba Collymore, Jimai Njodzeka, James Welch III, Sarah Andrews, and Alejandro Ochoa. Thanks for everything and for caring about this book as if it were your own.

Portions of chapter 3 first appeared, in a different form, as "The Haunting of a Nation: Ghostly Public Discourses and Jamaican National Trauma," in *The Supernatural Revamped: From Timeworn Legends to Twenty-First-Century Chic*, edited by Barbara Brodman and James E. Doan (Madison, NJ: Fairleigh Dickinson University Press, 2016), copublished by The Rowman & Littlefield Publishing Group, Inc., © 2016 by Rowman & Littlefield, all rights reserved.

Finally, heartfelt thanks to my husband, Dean, who stood on the sidelines and cheered me on, especially in the final few meters of the journey. Your love and support makes all the difference, husband.

Working Juju

INTRODUCTION

Kingdoms in Other Worlds
The Science of Working Juju

> Prohibited items are absolutely forbidden from entering Jamaica, some of which include ... all publications of de Laurence Scott and Company of Chicago in the United States of America relating to divination, magic, cultism or supernatural arts.
>
> "PROHIBITED ITEMS,"
> JAMAICA CUSTOMS AGENCY (2018)

The Caribbean has historically been constructed as a region mantled by the fantastic. Tales of the Maroon leader Nanny's mystical capacity to catch bullets with her buttocks, stories featuring mythological characters such as the cloven-hoofed temptress La Diablesse, and reports of sightings of the disruptive spirit known as a rolling calf are standard fare across the region. These discourses that proliferate within the Caribbean are supplemented by others created beyond Caribbean geographic and cultural boundaries. Planter-historian accounts of Obeah rituals among the enslaved, Hollywood's construction of the liminal zombie, and TV advertisements featuring the memorable Miss Cleo of the Psychic Readers Network all situate the Caribbean as an anomalous, irrational space. Miss Cleo was in many ways a purveyor of "juju"—a term commonly used in the Caribbean and in other parts of the African diaspora to mean a magical spell—and I perceive deployments of the fantastic such as those mentioned above as amounting to acts of discursive juju. I employ this term to indicate how constructions of the fantastical Caribbean conjure varied perceptions of the region.

Working Juju analyzes those imaginings and interrogates the freighting of Caribbean-infused spaces with characteristics that register as fantastical. These fantastical traits may be described as magical, supernatural, uncanny, paranormal, mystical, or speculative. *Working Juju* examines the politics of representation of the fantastic in fiction, nonfiction, film, folklore, the visual arts, and song. This project asks throughout, what are the discursive threads that run through texts featuring the Caribbean fantastic?

Working Juju particularly intends to tease out the multilayered and often obscured connections among these texts. Fantastical representations of the region generally occupy one of two spaces. In the first, the Caribbean fantastic facilitates an imagining of the colonial experience and its aftermath as one in which the region and its representatives exercise agency, and in which the humanity of the region's inhabitants is asserted. For example, the contemporary Caribbean science fiction writer Tobias Buckell's construction of futuristic, kick-ass Caribbean cyborgs sustains myths about Caribbean perseverance into a Caribbean future. Alternately, the fantastic is sometimes situated as a signifier of the irrational and uncivilized. This is the case with Edward Long's *The History of Jamaica*, published in 1774. The text portrays Afro-Caribbean spiritual practices in ways that indict the region for barbarity. The thread that unites portrayals of the fantastic Caribbean in these works is the tendency to locate Caribbean belief systems as powerful, sometimes in contradiction to the text's ideological posture. Despite the apparent chasm between Buckell's futuristic Caribbean landscape populated by cyborgs and Long's account of plantations full of foolhardy slaves, the texts share characteristics in their deployment of the fantastic and assert that Caribbean belief systems are sources of power and resilience.

Long's disparaging account, contrary to his narrative's apparent intention, situates Caribbean peoples as gritty, able to persevere and overcome against all odds. They believe in their capacity to transform their experience through their own agency in the midst of oppressive circumstances. This agency emerges from the portrayal of the Caribbean fantastic as a system that operates beyond the bounds of Western empirical knowledge and therefore cannot be explained or controlled by Western systems of belief. Long identifies these belief systems as the knowledge of Obeah that survived the transatlantic voyage, that is, as part of the cultural heritage of captured Africans. Buckell, on the other hand, ties these belief systems to historical notions of Caribbean self-determination and Caribbean-influenced political movements. For example, a group of spaceships manned by Caribbean-identified characters—crucial to the plot of his novels—is part of the original fleet from a company named the Black Starliner Corporation. This fleet transported Caribbean refugees to safety in a future world. The fleet's name invokes Marcus Garvey's shipping enterprise (the Black Star Line) and suggests that the fleet shares Garvey's mission of financial and social emancipation for the African diaspora.

Additionally, both texts show Caribbean peoples' belief in their own agency to be tenacious and unfettered, no matter the fragility or urgency of their situations, and suggest a rejection of Western or foreign epistemologies as superior. Buckell's and Long's works thus in many respects occupy the same fantastical literary landscape. Their discursive agility and the way their location of the fantastic results in multilayered meaning then become the ultimate act of "working juju." Accounts such as Long's, constructions of the fantastic meant to deliberately or inadvertently malign aspects of Caribbean identity and experience end up simultaneously and unwittingly situating Caribbean belief systems, peoples, and spaces as potent and rebellious antihegemonic forces.

Additionally, although Caribbean people often deploy the fantastic to highlight the region's legacy of imperialism and internal deterioration, and non-Caribbean agents often use the fantastic to pathologize the region and divert attention from the ravaging effects of slavery and colonialism, the nature of the representations from either group is not uniformly consistent. For example, the calypso performer Mighty Sparrow's song "Obeah Wedding" treats Afro-Caribbean spirituality as an anti-intellectual affront to modernity and as the province of foolish women such as the protagonist, Melda, who believes she can catch her man with the help of Obeah.[1] The song's mockery of Obeah is consistent with the view of the significant portion of the Caribbean population that rejects Afro-Caribbean spiritual practices, believing them to be uncivilized as well as contradictory to the belief systems of mainstream religions such as Christianity, Hinduism, and Islam.

This book also attends to the specific sociohistorical moment when a text was produced, recognizing that it likely influenced how the fantastic was deployed. The disparaging, reductive portrayals of Afro-Caribbean spiritual practices written by British planter-historians such as Edward Long participate in a Western conversation about an imagined Caribbean populated by foolish beings. For example, Long writes: "Not long since, some of these execrable wretches in Jamaica introduced what they called the myal dance, and established a kind of society, into which they invited all they could. The lure hung out was, that every Negroe, initiated into the myal society, would be invulnerable by the white men; and although they might in appearance be slain, the obeah-man could, at his pleasure, restore the body to life."[2] Long's *History of Jamaica* was written in the midst of intensifying debates about slavery and the slave trade, and his account of life on the plantations tried to show that Africans were incapable of self-governance and unsuitable candidates for freedom. On the other hand, Nanny's portrayal in Caribbean lore as the indefatigable heroine of the Maroons situates the Caribbean fantastic as a trope for resistance and rebellion. The legend of Nanny delivers a generative mythology about the survival of Africans in the New World as well as reassurances about the capacity of Caribbean peoples to resist oppressive forces.

Theoretical Influences

Numerous scholarly studies contemplate the Caribbean fantastic, but none of them uses expansive textual venues to the extent that this project does. Some studies focus on specific magico-religious spiritual practices such as Obeah and Vodun. Among these are nineteenth-century texts such as Henry Hesketh Bell's *Obeah: Witchcraft in the West Indies* and early twentieth-century texts such as Zora Neale Hurston's *Tell My Horse: Voodoo and Life in Haiti and Jamaica*. More recent studies include *Sacred Possessions: Vodou, Santería, Obeah, and the Caribbean*, by Margarite Fernández Olmos and Lizabeth Paravisini-Gebert; *The Cultural Politics of Obeah: Religion, Colonialism, and Modernity in the Caribbean World*, by Diana Paton; *Voodoo in Haiti*, by Alfred Métraux; and *Enacting Power: The Criminalization of Obeah in the Anglophone Caribbean, 1760–2011*, by Jerome S. Handler and Kenneth M. Bilby. Despite all the scholarly attention given to the Caribbean fantastic in its spiritual or religious aspect, few works engage with it in its many other manifestations. Aside from projects that analyze specific texts featuring the fantastic, only a few works, such as Giselle Anatol's *The Things That Fly in the Night*, address the fantastic in multiple textual forms.

The Things That Fly in the Night, an intriguing study of vampirism in the African diaspora, is a helpful point of reference for theorizing about the Caribbean supernatural. The study, in Anatol's words, "attempts to strip away the 'fat' and reveal the 'bone' beneath traditional and re-appropriated renderings of vampiric women in African diasporic—and particularly circum-Caribbean—narratives."[3] Furthermore, she contends that the "highly politicized trope of the vampire has been used for decades in the Caribbean and throughout the African diaspora to comment on the exploitation of colonized people and landscapes." My approach in *Working Juju* in many ways parallels Anatol's; both are interested in the aesthetics of representation and, more specifically, in the way in which the Caribbean fantastic engages with the colonial experience of the region. Anatol's analysis of female vampire stories from the diaspora "exposes a complicated web of relations and interactions between diasporic communities." In the same vein, I aim to explore the discursive threads connecting fantastical representations of the region. My approach resembles that of Anatol, who is concerned with the "conceptual paths" of Caribbean vampire stories and how these paths intersect and overlap.

Another Caribbean studies theorist whose work informs this study is Joan Dayan (now Colin Dayan). She posits an intimate connection between the atrocities of the colonial experience in the Caribbean and the fantastic: "I am suggesting that we connect remembered torture with oppressive magic. Phantoms of domination and scenes of the past return, transmogrified and reinvested with new meanings."[4] Dayan's analysis specifically refers to connections she observes between Caribbean myths about creatures that shed their skin and the cruel punishment of slaves on Saint-Domingue who were whipped until their skin lifted to expose their flesh. Substances such as salt and pepper, which would cause agonizing pain, were then applied to open wounds in horrific acts of torture.[5] *Working Juju* engages in a sustained consideration of the relationship between the fantastic and regional traumas.

Mimi Sheller's study *Consuming the Caribbean: From Arawaks to Zombies* also helped shape the theoretical scaffolding of this project. Sheller situates consumption as a trope for the predacious relationship between western Europe and North America, on the one hand, and the Caribbean on the other. These larger regions, Sheller argues, "have unceasingly consumed the natural environment, commodities, human bodies, and cultures of the Caribbean over the past five hundred years."[6] This act of consuming landscapes and their inhabitants evokes the idea of the monster. Just as Sheller employs the concept of this fantastical creature as a cohering principle for her study, I rely on the mobilization of the concept of the fantastic in general as a theoretical motif in *Working Juju*. In the oft-cited *Specters of Marx: The State of the Debt, the Work of Mourning, and the New International*, Jacques Derrida uses the fantastic to propel his discussion. He relies throughout on the idea of hauntings, treating a spectral presence as a figurative representation of history.[7] Derrida states that the decision to "learn to *live* with ghosts" is a choice to live "more justly" and to embrace history's incursions into the present. Derrida's reading of spectral encounters as a means by which history searches for redress is yet another example of how the fantastic can inform critical discussions.

Justification of the Corpus

While cultural engagement with the fantastic occurs across several language groups in the Caribbean, the texts I discuss in *Working Juju* are in English. This is a matter of expediency: English is my language of fluency. More specifically, the Caribbean countries on which this project focuses are primarily Jamaica and Haiti (as is the case with Zora Neale Hurston's popular study *Tell My Horse*). People from outside the Caribbean have historically not distinguished between Vodun (associated with Haiti) and Obeah (Jamaica), and the frequent collapsing of the identities of these practices has strongly associated the two nations. Additionally, research materials that yielded the richest opportunities to explore the Caribbean fantastic in discourses originating from outside of the region often pertained to Haiti and Jamaica. For example, works written by planter-historians (discussed in chapter 1) focus a good deal on Jamaica, and travel narratives and articles in the popular media about Haiti served as important contributions to the creation of a discursive architecture of the region in relation to the fantastic, painting the region as a bizarre and unpredictable space.

Fantastical discourses about Haiti emerged in tandem with its founding as a nation-state, and commentary linking Haiti with the supernatural has served as the basis for arguments recommending America's strategic intervention in Haiti's affairs. Born from the 1791 slave rebellion led by Toussaint

Louverture in the French Caribbean colony of Saint-Domingue, Haiti became, in 1804, the first black republic in the New World. America's relationship with Haiti was troubled from the latter's establishment, unsteadied by the former's anxiety about the emergence of a free black republic only seven hundred miles away. As Michael Dash explains, "Haitian independence challenged the whole system of slavery and notions of black inferiority," and "the fear of slave insurrection ran deep in the white American imagination in the nineteenth century."[8] As a result, the United States refused to recognize Haiti until 1862. According to Dash, the discursive result of America's fear and suspicion was its persistent "mythification" of Haiti and its construction of the nation as "other." As an early example, Dash cites the journalist William Boyce, who around 1900 argued for an American intervention in Haiti because of that country's "horrible form of sorcery with its cannibalistic rites."[9] Dash also mentions Frederick Ober's *In the Wake of Columbus*, published in 1893, which similarly calls for the United States to intervene in Haiti, "take this irresponsible island republic in hand, and administer to it a salutary lesson." This characterization of Haiti as bizarre and mythic, Dash argues, "would guarantee a constant stream of researchers, missionaries, adventurers and tourists with a taste for the outlandish," bent on experiencing Haiti's "predetermined strangeness." Other discourses have similarly recommended Haiti's strangeness.

For example, an article titled "Cannibals in Hayti," published by *Harper's Weekly* in September 1865, claims that there had been a recent resurgence of a cannibalistic "voodoo" sect: "The devotees begin their horrid festival by an act of cannibalism. The monsters, after having stuffed and devoured one unfortunate child, were about to gormondize [*sic*] upon a second victim when justice overtook them."[10] These early discourses closely associating cannibalism with Afro-Caribbean spirituality suggest that the two are interchangeable and equally barbaric expressions of the Haitian character. In *Haiti's Bad Press*, Robert Lawless surveys a range of condemnatory publications about Haiti and argues that "most of the works on Haiti that the public reads are based on myths, most of which are, at best, uninformed and plagiaristic and, at worst, mean-spirited and narrow-minded."[11] He cites a telling example in a December 1920 *National Geographic* article: "Here, in the elemental wilderness, the natives rapidly forgot their thin veneer of Christian civilization and reverted to utter, unthinking animalism, swayed only by fear of local bandit chiefs and the black magic of voodoo witch doctors."[12] The discursive manifestation of this association between Haiti and the outlandish is particularly evident in texts (both literary and filmic) produced during the American occupation of Haiti, 1915–34. The occupation was preceded by U.S. anxieties over Haiti's political and economic stability.[13] These included concerns about the disproportionate amount of economic influence wielded by Haiti's small German population (World War I was raging at the time), Haiti's ability to pay its national debt (which, some argued, was an unfounded worry), and the security of American interests in Haiti; for the most part, however, strategic military concerns led to the occupation.[14] While the political and economic impact of consistently portraying Haiti, indeed the entire region, as shrouded in a mist of strangeness may seem to only render the region as quirky, Sarah Lauro argues that "accusations of cannibalism, the practice of dark magic, and even rumors of raising the dead justified various interventions and occupations of foreign lands," including Haiti.[15]

Films such as *White Zombie* (1932), *King of the Zombies* (1941), and *I Walked with a Zombie* (1943) are useful examples of how Haiti was portrayed in and around the period of the occupation. These films feature white women who fall helpless prey to voodoo while visiting Haiti (constructed as a strange and malevolent space), and in the process become transformed into zombies. Literary texts from this period display a similar penchant for constructing Haiti as bizarre, unstable, and otherworldly. According to Joan Dayan, "It should not surprise us that during the American occupation, from 1915 to 1934, tales of cannibalism, torture, and zombies were published in [the United States]. What better way to justify the 'civilizing' presence of marines in Haiti than to project the phantasm of barbarism."[16] Dayan argues further that "representations of vodoun have usually served a political purpose."[17] Making a similar argument, Michael Dash cites a variety of books, including John Houston Craige's *Cannibal Cousins* (1934), Faustin Wirkus's *The White King of La Gonave* (1931), and William Seabrook's *Magic Island* (1929) as examples of occupation literature written by Americans that constructs Haiti as bizarre. According to Dash, "We can divide American commentators into two broad categories: apologists for the Occupation and defenders of Negro primitivism." He further explains that these texts were intent on constructing Haiti as "different from the rest of the world"; and though they might "differ on the nature of this difference," they "shared a taste for the theatrical and the melodramatic that ensured their commercial appeal."[18]

A good deal of this supposed strangeness had to do with the supernatural. For example, in his travel narrative *The Magic Island*, William Seabrook offers a titillating account of Haitian culture. He portrays himself as an intrepid, blood-guzzling adventurer intrigued by what he perceives as the Haitians' uninhibited and authentic spiritual transactions, which provide a vital contrast with the cold, soulless religious practices of the West. As he participates in his own "blood baptism" ceremony and observes the sacrifice of a goat, Seabrook declares: "Better a black papaloi in Haiti with blood-stained hands who believes in his living gods than a frock-coated minister on Fifth Avenue reducing Christ to a solar myth and rationalizing the Immaculate Conception."[19] Seabrook underpins his narrative with other reproaches of Western culture, suggesting that spiritual practices like Vodun occupy a morally superior space because they are less circumscribed and more organic than Christianity. Despite his generally charitable disposition toward Haitian culture, Seabrook nevertheless describes his time in Haiti as an encounter with the bizarre.

This characterization of Haiti has historically deflected attention from Haiti's most prevalent problems, and continues to do so. The persistence of this mythification was apparent in the aftermath of the 2010 earthquake in Haiti, when commentary as strange as the strangeness it perpetuated circulated through the media by way of questions regarding whether "voodoo" was in some way accountable for the earthquake as well as other moments of crisis in that country. This inflammatory and accusatory rhetoric issued predominantly from the Christian Right.

Perhaps the most widely repeated comment of this nature came from the televangelist Pat Robertson, who in response to the earthquake claimed that Haiti was "cursed." While raising funds for earthquake disaster relief on an episode of the Christian Broadcasting Network's *The 700 Club*, Robertson unequivocally assigned blame for the earthquake to Haiti's revolutionary history: "Something happened a long time ago in Haiti, and people might not want to talk about it. They were under the heel of the French. You know, Napoleon III, or whatever. And they got together and swore a pact to the devil. They said, we will serve you if you'll get us free from the French. True story. And so, the devil said, okay it's a deal."[20] Permutations of Robertson's claim that Haiti had plunged into an abyss of evil was echoed repeatedly in the weeks that followed the earthquake.

In a *Washington Post* article titled "Does God Hate Haiti?," published on January 20, 2010, R. Albert Mohler Jr., president of the Southern Baptist Theological Seminary, endorses Robertson's perspective and suggests that the earthquake was God's vengeance against Haiti for its practice of voodoo: "In truth, it is hard not to describe the earthquake as a disaster of biblical proportions. It certainly looks as if the wrath of God has fallen upon the Caribbean nation. Add to this the fact that Haiti is well known for its history of religious syncretism—mixing elements of various faiths, including occult practices. The nation is known for voodoo, sorcery, and a Catholic tradition that has been greatly influenced by the occult."[21] Mohler goes on to suggest that the Haitian Revolution was the spawn of "a pact with the Devil to throw off the French" and that somehow the revolution was in fact a faceoff between good and evil, light and darkness, the sacred and the profane. Mohler implies that although the devil may appear to have won, God has been getting payback ever since: "Thus, some would use that tradition [of practicing voodoo] to explain all that has marked the tragedy of Haitian history—including now the earthquake of January 12, 2010." Statements like this make it apparent that Mohler cannot respond in the affirmative to the question that titles his article, "Does God Hate Haiti?," and instead he prevaricates via a series of rhetorical questions. Mohler writes, "Does God hate Haiti?" and then states, "God hates sin, and will punish both individual sinners and nations." He also asks, "Will God judge Haiti for its spiritual darkness?" And of course, he answers, "Of course."

Robertson's and Mohler's comments maintain the construction of Haiti as outlandish, a nation teetering on the boundary between the real world and a haunted kingdom infiltrated by fallen angels, a perspective that benefits the Christian Right because it confirms its claim that God punishes "evildoers." Furthermore, Mohler describes this "pact with the Devil" as a "tradition," suggesting that the revolution was only the beginning of Haiti's ongoing pursuit of an alliance with the diabolical forces of the world.

Hardly enough can be said about Robertson's and Mohler's racist, historically incorrect (for example, the French ruler at the time of the revolution was Napoleon Bonaparte, not Napoleon III), and simplistic analysis of the Haitian Revolution. In these cases as well as in every other instance in which

Vodun and its role in the Haitian Revolution are designated as agents of Haiti's misfortunes, we are plunged back into the tradition of American discourses that associate Haiti with the bizarre and distract attention from the most relevant problems at hand.[22] Furthermore, Vodun had a foundational role in the Haitian Revolution and the ceremony believed to have initiated the now-legendary revolt. C. L. R. James explains the ritualistic underpinnings of the uprising when he describes its launch: "Their priests . . . chanted the wanga, and the women and children sang and danced in a frenzy. When these had reached the necessary height of excitement the fighters attacked."[23] Hans Schmidt argues that in Haiti, Vodun has functioned as a "rallying point for mass political action and resistance against foreign domination"—for example, "During the guerilla war against the United States Marines in 1919, Haitian soldiers, often conspicuous for their bravery, went into battle wearing vodoun charms . . . thought to ward off enemy bullets."[24] Both James's and Schmidt's accounts suggest that Vodun was a potent source of inspiration at key moments in Haiti's resistance against hegemonic forces.

Rhetorical strategies to render Vodun fraudulent and hollow reflect a refusal to give legitimacy to the spiritual practice at the core of Haiti's liberation and perhaps ultimately suggest the persistence of America's historical reluctance to recognize and legitimize the first black republic in the New World. The pervasive suggestion that Vodun, the bolstering force at the soul of the Haitian Revolution, is bankrupt and a sham—or as Robertson and Mohler claim, rooted in evil and sorcery—is a reaffirmation of black primitivism, indicting not only Haiti but also the rest of the Caribbean and, I would argue, the entire African diaspora, because it calls into question the ability of black people to engage in effective self-governance. This rendering of Vodun implies further that any act to claim or reclaim black sovereignty is necessarily founded in evil or, at best, some barren system of belief.

In contrast to these derogatory perceptions of Haiti, the Cuban novelist Alejo Carpentier, who coined the term *lo real maravilloso Americano* (the marvelous American reality) in the introduction to his 1949 novel *The Kingdom of This World*, asserts Haiti's profound importance to the region, specifically its impact on him and his conceptualization of the Caribbean. Additionally, Carpentier articulates the transformative role that a 1940s visit to Haiti had on the emergence of his concept of the marvelous real.[25] In relation to his visit, he notes the inspiring power of Vodun beliefs: "I was in a land where thousands of men, anxious for freedom, believed in Mackandal's lycanthropic powers to the extent that their collective faith produced a miracle on the day of his execution. I had already heard the prodigious story of Bouckman, the Jamaican initiate."[26] Makandal, a *houngan*, or Vodun priest, supposedly able to transform himself into various animals, led a slave revolt in Haiti in 1757.[27] Makandal's crusade against the Haitian plantocracy is acknowledged as having prepared the foundation for the revolution and for emergence of Dutty Boukman, the Jamaican who led the ceremony at Bois-Caïman that initiated the revolution.[28] The scene at Bois-Caïman in 1791 was rooted in an esoteric Caribbean, and Boukman led his followers in a ritual that promised to give them mythical abilities informed by Makandal's legacy and reputed fantastical powers. The scene at Bois-Caïman epitomizes the connection between Haiti and Jamaica, countries with a rich history of beliefs in fantastical possibilities and with legacies of resistance. That history and those legacies attracted inordinate levels of surveillance and misrepresentation from colonizing powers terrified by what the epistemological roots of these belief systems suggested about the possibilities of black political agency.

Additionally, evocations of the Caribbean fantastic in U.S. popular and literary culture seem to quite often emerge in relation to Haiti and Jamaica. As a scholar living in the United States, I usually find this cultural landscape to be the most relevant point of reference for discussions of contemporary American discourses about the region. Among countries in the region, Haiti and Jamaica have had their cultures most visibly appropriated and ascribed to the realm of the fantastic. While Santeria, an Afro-Caribbean spiritual practice most closely associated with Cuba, has been featured in literature, film, and television, representations of Obeah and Vodun seem to be the Caribbean spiritualities most often featured in American popular culture. Examples include the portrayal of the Obeah woman Tia Dalma in the *Pirates of the Caribbean* franchise, whose first installation is set in Jamaica during the time of slavery (see chapter 2). Appropriations of Vodun, often referred to as "voodoo," are also common fare in American cinema and television, including early zombie films set in the Caribbean and countless TV shows and horror movies featuring "voodoo" priestesses, such as *American Horror Story: Coven*, the third season of the television anthology.

The prominence of these nations in global discourses about the region is understandable because of their comparatively large populations. Haiti, which shares the island of Hispaniola with its neighbor, the Dominican Republic, was the largest of France's colonies in the Caribbean and remains the second-most populous nation in the region, behind Cuba. Jamaica, which was Britain's largest Caribbean colony in population, remains the largest English-speaking Caribbean nation. For these reasons and others, the hypervisibility of Haiti and Jamaica on the international cultural and political landscape is not a recent phenomenon. In addition to the financial value of these countries to their colonizers, they attracted attention based on the threat they posed to European dominance in the region. France's worst anxieties surrounding Haiti materialized with the success of the Haitian Revolution, and Jamaica's frequent revolts caused Britain ongoing trouble. Mary Reckord outlines these repeated insurrections: "Violent protest against slavery in the form of riot or rebellion had been endemic in eighteenth-century Jamaica; the outbreaks occurred on average every five years, and two such efforts, the Maroon wars of 1738 and 1795, secured freedom for small communities of ex-slaves in the mountain districts."[29]

According to Diana Paton, anxiety about Obeah and slave uprisings among the Jamaican plantocracy was particularly influenced by the island's reliance on the ongoing importation of Africans: "It seems likely that their [planters'] awareness of this dependence drove their greater anxiety about the power of Africans, expressed through their concern about Obeah."[30] Paton also explains that "it was the Obeah man's disruption of the supposedly natural lines of authority and dependence between planter and slave that the Jamaicans found most disturbing about Obeah." Perhaps the attention that these countries attracted as threats to the colonial project, in addition to the association of their magico-religious practices with the undermining of colonial power, has sustained their hypervisibility into the twenty-first century. This visibility, I suggest, has a role in the frequent appropriation of these practices in the global cultural landscape.

The hypervisibility of Haiti and Jamaica influenced my choice of texts to analyze for this project. I discuss travel writing about the two countries. The main visual artists whose work I describe are Haitian; the songs I discuss and the development of the "science" tradition in Obeah center on Jamaica. The films I critique feature characters and cultural practices strongly associated with Haiti and Jamaica, and the chapter on ghost stories focuses on a specific set of reported hauntings in Jamaica during the mid-twentieth century as the nation barreled toward independence. It was important to cover a range of cultural categories and historical periods in order to fully explore perceptions of Haiti and Jamaica in relation to the fantastic. Furthermore, anchoring the research in multiple genres provided added opportunities to identify discursive threads across modes of representation.

While texts associated with Jamaica and Haiti receive primary attention in *Working Juju*, chapter 4, the most extended literary analysis in the study, departs from that scheme. Focused entirely on the work of the Grenadian science fiction writer Tobias Buckell, it explores his Xenowealth series, which is set in a futuristic Caribbean space. While the works of many well-known Caribbean writers partake of the literary fantastic, including Edgar Mittelholzer, Wilson Harris, Simone Schwarz-Bart, Patrick Chamoiseau, Erna Brodber, and Nalo Hopkinson, I am particularly interested in emerging writers such as Karen Lord and Tiphanie Yanique. To that end, I chose three of Buckell's novels with Caribbean-inspired themes and characters and stories informed by Caribbean history as a focus for this project, for a particular set of reasons. First, science fiction is a fascinating genre, and one of the more recent types of Caribbean writing to emerge. When this project was coalescing, I noticed a lack of scholarship on Buckell's texts, and I rarely came across presentations on his work at scholarly conferences. Finally, my presentations on him attracted a range of questions about who he was and what else he had written.

Other chapters include short discussions of works from other parts of the Caribbean. For example, chapter 3 briefly refers to stories from St. Lucia about small mythical creatures known as "boloms." The inclusion of texts from Caribbean lands other than Haiti or Jamaica—including Buckell's work—reflects writers' and artists' varying but consistent engagement with the fantastic across the Caribbean, a diversity that contributes to this project's arguments.

The complex relationship between the Caribbean and the fantastic can be seen in the Caribbean "science" tradition as well as in the region's cultural productions. This term refers to practices associated with Afro-Caribbean spirituality, particularly those anchored in the belief that people can acquire and exercise magical abilities with the aid of products and spells. As noted earlier, though the deployment of the fantastic from within the region often helps expose the Caribbean's legacy of imperialism and internal deterioration, and its activation from external actors often pathologizes the region, these representations are sometimes inconsistent with the cultural space of their origins. Some in the Caribbean turn their backs on Afro-Caribbean spiritual practices, believing them to oppose mainstream religious beliefs. Nonetheless, the Caribbean science tradition has fostered a space where Afro-Caribbean spiritual practices can be reconciled with the doctrines of Christianity.

The denigration of science work is evident in a number of reggae and calypso songs that refer to Obeah and its practitioners and, like "Obeah Wedding," use lyrical mockery and humor to situate the practice as both malevolent and ineffectual, reflecting a pervasive Caribbean ideological posture toward Obeah. Examples include Admiral Bailey's "Science Again," Yellow Man's "Nuh Tie Me," Mighty Sparrow's "Witch Doctor," and Lovindeer's "The Oil." Kenneth Bilby explains that in Jamaica, Protestant Christian belief saw Obeah as a form of "iniquity," a view influencing the current representation of the practice: "It is not surprising, then, that the majority of songs referencing obeah in the Anglophone Caribbean are populated with workers of iniquity of one kind or another. One of the more common images of obeah in popular music is as a kind of antisocial witchcraft or sorcery."[31] In Lovindeer's "The Oil," the narrator is engaged in a form of sorcery, promoting a broad range of Obeah-derived antidotes for life's troubles. He is versed in helping clients circumvent obstacles and enhance their mobility via a number of humorously titled potions. To address economic mobility there are "oil of make you get promotion," "oil of make you get U.S. visa," and even a product specially designed for politicians: "oil of collect taxes from ganja." In the domain of romance, there is an equally compelling range of oils: "oil of make hard-to-get gal surrender," "oil of make man stop girly, girly," and the remarkable "oil of make ugly man look handsome." The science-man narrator of the song even has oils that can help clients overcome the obstacle of physiological blackness, such as "oil of make a knotty hair get curly" and "oil of make black gal get brown baby." Lovindeer's song highlights the Caribbean science tradition, an important part of the Obeah complex that features the use of manufactured substances such as oils, powders, and candles.

Mighty Sparrow's song "Witch Doctor" offers a similar take on the science tradition, making humorous, tongue-in-cheek references to popular presumptions about what is in the science worker's arsenal of tools, such as "a living bat," "a little white rat," "an eagle's claw" and a "rabbit's paw."[32] The song's narrator, the titular witch doctor, boasts of his skills at manipulating the world with the aid of the fantastic. "Witch Doctor" derides the practice of Obeah by mockingly using terms like "abracadabra," merging Obeah with sleight-of-hand entertainment magic, and by suggesting that commonplace substances such as graveyard dirt and donkey's blood can enhance sexual fulfillment. According to the narrator, "If things go fine," with the spells he is casting, "every woman going to be mine."

One of the leading influencers of science practitioners like those depicted in Lovindeer's and Sparrow's songs was Lauron William de Laurence, an American occultist who came to prominence in the early twentieth century. The references to magical formulas and spells in the songs I discuss are very closely associated with de Laurence. The belief in spells and formulas forms one pole of Caribbean attitudes toward the fantastic, and disparaging commentary on science workers forms the other.

De Laurence's catalogue of books and magical artifacts was extremely popular in the Caribbean and other parts of the diaspora, and his approach to spirituality inspired an entirely new branch of Obeah in Jamaica. Owen Davies's study *Grimoires: A History of Magic Books* offers an extensive discussion of de Laurence's life.[33] A white man from Cleveland, de Laurence began his career in the occult as a door-to-door salesman of books on the subject of hypnotism and psychology. Enamored of hypnosis, he later studied it and then offered lessons in it; in 1900, he opened a hypnotism school in Chicago. A few years later, he started a publishing business, De Laurence, Scott and Company, which brought out a range of books on magic and the occult. He eventually added an extensive mail-order catalogue of paranormal products such as "invocation candles," talismans, and magical jewelry.

While De Laurence enjoyed incredible popularity and financial success, his career was plagued with legal issues, culminating in charges by the U.S. Post Office of "conducting a scheme for obtaining money through the mail by means of false pretenses, representations and promises."[34] According to Davies, he repeatedly plagiarized and pirated texts, sometimes claiming authorship of material he had stolen word-for-word from other authors. A

1919 trial revealed that besides claiming authorship or editorial input over texts that he had not written, he was woefully unfamiliar with the content of books he had purportedly written; according to Davies, he in fact was generally ignorant of the genre of books in which he traded. Despite legal difficulties in the United States, he was extremely popular in the African American community, West Africa, and, especially, the Caribbean. According to Davies, "De Laurence was and is respected in West Africa but in the Caribbean he achieved mythical status."

In all these regions, his book *The Sixth and Seventh Books of Moses* had a particularly profound influence on spiritual practices.[35] In *Other Books, Other Powers*, Patrick Polk contends that *The Sixth and Seventh Books of Moses* was "perhaps the most influential gnostic volume within the Afro-Atlantic cultural continuum."[36] Polk's comment helps illuminate the significance of de Laurence's publication across the diaspora. According to Davies, de Laurence's books had a role in the growth of Mami Wata worship in Nigeria and the "'De-laurencification' of medical traditions" in Cameroon.[37] In Trinidad, Davies notes, "*The Sixth and Seventh Books of Moses* was almost certainly the inspiration for the various 'spiritual' symbols used in Spiritual Baptist ritual worship." But, he argues, "nowhere in the Caribbean did De Laurence have a more profound social influence than in Jamaica," where his products shaped Obeah practices as well as Rastafarianism. So significant was his impact that laws banning his books were enacted in Jamaica and other parts of the Caribbean. In Jamaica the Undesirable Publications Law of 1940 made it an offence "either to import, to publish, to sell, to distribute, to reproduce, or without lawful excuse to be in possession of . . . All publications of De Laurence Scott and Company of Chicago in the United States of America relating to divination, occultism, supernatural arts or other esoteric subjects." This ban on his publications is indicative of their popularity at the time the law was passed. Curiously enough, his books remain among the prohibited items listed on the Jamaica Customs website, alongside "indecent and obscene prints."[38]

The anxiety generated in Jamaica and other parts of the Caribbean by de Laurence's publications was due to their tremendous popularity, which seems to have derived, at least in part, from how he fashioned himself and his products. Integral to de Laurence's success were the personas that he assumed. When he first began offering hypnotism lessons, he titled himself

"Professor," for which he later substituted "Doctor" when he began to present himself as a Hindu mystic.[39] An ad placed in the Jamaican newspaper the *Daily Gleaner* on August 30, 1939, promotes the de Laurence company's catalogue. The ad lists a number of products available for order, including "Books on Caballistic and Ceremonial Magic . . . Spirit Scrolls, Magic Mirrors, Transcendental Magic, and Oriental Perfumes." The ad features images of de Laurence clad in a robe, his head bound in a turban and a wand protruding from one hand.

De Laurence's effort to construct himself as an Asian mystic was part of a larger undertaking to shape his persona into a "Hindu swami."[40] De Laurence's ad implies that his products offer an early twentieth-century form of "high-tech" magic, a magic that no longer relied on natural ingredients but on synthetic products such as candles and incense that were commercialized and packaged for easy accessibility. The decision to style himself as an Eastern mystic and associate himself and his products with Hinduism through his clothing, publications, and the name of his institute was part of a trend among occultists at that time. In the essay "The Hindu in Hoodoo," Philip Deslippe provides the background for this phenomenon: "For decades leading up to the Great Migration, and well back into the nineteenth century, the wider American perception of India and Hinduism, and by extension, yoga as a form of mental magic, was taking shape through a web of science, politics, religion, and popular culture. In true Orientalist fashion, religion in India was grossly distorted into an imagined circus of idol worshiping and widow burning that was deployed as a representation of an exotic other to help establish the supremacy of Christianity in the civilized West."[41] Entrepreneurial occultists like de Laurence made good commercial use of these perceptions, which, as Deslippe explains, were widespread in the United States: "Starting as early as the late nineteenth century, there were legions of vaudeville magicians, stage hypnotists, and fortune tellers who capitalized on these perceptions and fanned out across the United States, using Orientalized personas to create an exotic allure for their audiences that played on the dominant popular American understanding of yogis as wonder-workers with fantastic mental powers."

To "Other" himself while marketing to communities already Othered because of race and geography, de Laurence had to invent and invoke alternate, magical colored bodies and new, fantastical geographies. Hence, his ad implies that the source of his magic potency rests in Asia, which he constructs as exotic and unknown in the way that the Caribbean has historically been constructed as exotic and unknown and associated with the mysterious. De Laurence's marketing strategy was significant because it highlighted how even within an Othered subaltern population, the further Othering of a persona associated with the supernatural could enhance its potency in the realm of the fantastic. In de Laurence's case, his advertisement sought to suggest that as an Eastern mystic, he was well positioned to offer enhanced access to the spirit world.

De Laurence marks himself and his products as strange and unknowable in the way that historical conversations about the Caribbean have marked the region as strange and unknowable. Despite de Laurence's trafficking in the expediencies of racial identity to promote his business, and despite the ongoing rejection of Obeah in some Caribbean spaces, the science tradition served an important role in providing a space for the consolidation of Obeah with the tenets of Christianity. In fact, Polk explains that in relation to the African-derived American spiritual practice of hoodoo, *The Sixth and Seventh Books of Moses* "help[ed] to integrate biblical scripture into a ritual system that remains largely of African derivation."[42] Polk points out that the integration of these spiritual systems addressed believers' common adversities: "Adherents of African American spiritual traditions such as Vodou, Obeah, and Hoodoo have . . . co-opted and adapted available metaphysical resources as part of the process of creating integrated belief systems that reflect and address the emotional, environmental, and social realities faced by adherents on a daily basis." De Laurence and the science tradition he influenced remain objects of ridicule in many Caribbean discursive arenas, such as popular music; but this rejection disregards the valuable ways in which science men and women helped open a space in the Caribbean for the retention of Afro-Atlantic cultural traditions within the ideological boundaries of Christianity. For example, Polk notes the significant iconographic role of Moses in the Afro-Caribbean community as an emblem of hope and the possibility of prevailing over tribulation.

This complex relationship between de Laurence and the region exemplifies the sometimes convoluted ways in which the fantastic functions in the Caribbean. The mythos of the science worker as irrelevant and disruptive, reflected in the songs I discuss, is belied by the important continuities the science tradition has accommodated, allowing Afro-Caribbean spiritual practices like Obeah to align with modernity and transform themselves as new technologies became available in the early twentieth century. It is acts of juju such as these that this study pursues—the ways in which cultural artifacts within the orbit of the Caribbean fantastic participate in or reveal processes of mutation and transmogrification that offer new understandings of the region.

Notes on Terminology

Throughout this book, I use the concept of the "fantastic" to indicate an occurrence, a spiritual practice, an individual characteristic, or an ability that defies an explanation anchored in empirical knowledge. Terms that indicate the fantastic include the following: magical, supernatural, paranormal, uncanny, mystical, and (specifically in relation to fiction) speculative. All these refer to what one might consider representations of out-of-the-ordinary experiences that push against the boundaries of reality. While the terms vary slightly in meaning, and some of them overlap, they all point towards experiences that are in some way unexpected and that trouble the perception of reality. For example, "paranormal" is defined as "not scientifically explainable," but it is often substitutable for "supernatural," which is defined as "departing from what is usual or normal especially so as to appear to transcend the laws of nature" or "attributed to an invisible agent (such as a ghost or spirit)."[43] The term "speculative fiction" most often points toward what might be described as "a super category for all genres that deliberately depart from imitating 'consensus reality' of everyday experience."[44] It may include "sci-fi," "ghost stories," "post-apocalyptic fiction," and "superhero tales," to name only a few subgenres. These terms reflect the diversity in cosmological perspectives that this project considers, since in some communities the "paranormal" and the "mystical" are the normal. My use of these terms in some ways privileges Western epistemologies as the standard and relegates everything else to a variation. But since the larger cultural and political milieu in which I write and publish is heavily influenced by a Western worldview, there is a need to meet readers where they are, in order to expose alternate ways of seeing the world and comprehending expressions of the fantastic.

"The fantastic" is the broadest umbrella term for a range of characteristics generally considered fantastical, and it applies to a variety of texts. My use of the term expands upon Tzvetan Todorov's use of it to define a subgenre of literature. In *The Fantastic: A Structural Approach to a Literary Genre*, Todorov defines the fantastic as follows:

> The fantastic requires the fulfillment of three conditions. First, the text must oblige the reader to consider the world of the characters as a world of living persons and to hesitate between a natural or supernatural explanation of the events described. Second, this hesitation may also be experienced by a character; thus the reader's role is so to speak entrusted to a character, and at the same time the hesitation is represented, it becomes one of the themes of the work—in the case of naive reading, the actual reader identifies himself with the character. Third, the reader must adopt a certain attitude with regard to the text: he will reject allegorical as well as "poetic" interpretations.[45]

Todorov more succinctly explains "the heart of the fantastic" as follows: "In a world which is indeed our world, the one we know, a world without devils, sylphides, or vampires, there occurs an event which cannot be explained by the laws of this same familiar world."

Todorov's definition suggests that the fantastic presents somewhat as the ordinary, and aside from a moment of pause by both the reader and the characters in the text, the fantastical phenomenon is accepted as a real occurrence—not as a metaphor for something else. My use of the term "fantastic" ventures beyond the scope of literature and includes a more expansive range of texts (in music, painting, and the like) featuring a fantastical element that is for the most part treated as commonplace.

An idea related to the fantastic is magical realism, which strongly supports the conceptual framework of this study. Magical realism in fiction is defined as "a literary genre or style associated especially with Latin America that incorporates fantastic or mythical elements into otherwise realistic fiction."[46] The German art critic Franz Roh coined the term in 1925 (as *Magischer Realismus*) in reference to the visual arts.[47] The magical-realist style later took root among Latin American writers, including the Cuban novelist Alejo Carpentier, who, as previously noted, wrote about the concept *lo real maravilloso Americano* (the marvelous American reality) in the introduction to his 1949 novel *The Kingdom of This World*.[48] His visit to Haiti caused him to reach a new understanding of the fantastic, propelling his engagement with this idea into profound and authentic territory: "My first inkling of the marvelous real . . . came to me when, near the end of 1943, I was lucky enough to visit Henri Christophe's kingdom." (Christophe was a leader of the Haitian Revolution.) Carpentier's discovery revitalized him: "After having felt the undeniable spell of the lands of Haiti . . . I was moved to set this recently experienced marvelous reality beside the tiresome pretension of creating the marvelous that has characterized certain European literatures over the past thirty years."[49]

Carpentier goes on to complain that the visual arts in Europe had become stilted because of artists' reliance on unnatural and methodic features—"The result of willing the marvelous or any other trance is that the dream technicians become bureaucrats"—and so their artworks were nothing more than "a junkyard of sugar-coated watches." For Carpentier, Haiti undid these obstacles to creating complex, multilayered productions of the marvelous, and he describes himself during his visit as having "daily contact with something that could be defined as the marvelous real."[50]

Despite this early association with Haiti, magical realism has primarily been associated with literary works from Latin America, though critical scholarship anchored in magical realism is now global in scope.[51] Although the standard definition of magical realism suggests that the fantastic elements of a text are not disruptive and flow seamlessly into the text's reality, for many of the texts I engage with, the fantastical elements are disruptive and unsettling. This can be seen in the case of the Obeah practitioners on the plantation described in Long's work, the hauntings in Jamaica, and the uncanny creatures in Asser Saint-Val's paintings. These fantastical features disrupt the texts in which they are situated and often represent a clash of cosmologies.

While most often associated with literature, magical realism also appears in genres such as art and film. The term, however, was not ideal for use in this project, because its widely perceived function as a critical lens for discussing Latin American works would perhaps hobble it as a suitable approach for talking about Afro-Caribbean culture, in spite of its inspirational origins in Haiti. The term's ongoing association with Latin America has often been the source of tensions about the suitability of its use for works emerging from outside that region, and such disagreements burden the terminology in distracting ways. For example, the award-winning South African writer Zakes Mda outright rejects its application to his work: "Some critics have called my work magic realism. They say it was influenced by Latin-Americans. But I must tell you that the Latin-Americans have nothing to do with my work. First of all they did not invent the mode of magic realism. They merely popularized it."[52] My expanded version of Todorov's definition of the fantastic is relieved of the specific cultural and regional yokings of magical realism and the associated tensions.

An Orthographic Note

I use the spelling "Vodun" to refer to the popular Afro-Caribbean spiritual practice emerging out of Haiti. In the media it is often rendered as "voodoo," a term that has come to bear derogative presumptions about this practice. I capitalize Vodun, as I would any spiritual practice. I do not capitalize "voodoo," since the understanding of this term does not offer an accurate representation of the practice and carries a reductive connotation. I use "voodoo" sparingly and only to reflect the ideological perspective of others.

Chapter Outline

Chapter 1, "British Obeah: The Making of Caribbean Savages," examines eighteenth- and nineteenth-century British texts including *The History of Jamaica* by Edward Long, *The History, Civil and Commercial, of the British Colonies in the West Indies* by Bryan Edwards, and *Journal of a West India Proprietor* by Matthew "Monk" Lewis. These nonfiction texts contributed to European attempts to describe, explain, and quantify the region, making it knowable within the boundaries of Europe's intellectual framework. Additionally, I discuss how the historical moment during which these texts were produced influenced them.

Chapter 2, "Devilish Divas and Gangster Monsters: Hollywood's Monstrous Imaginings of the Caribbean," looks closely at Hollywood's representation of the Caribbean in films that feature a fantastical element. In addition, the chapter examines how Caribbean "monsters" are framed by the movie camera and what those framing strategies seem to suggest about the region and its inhabitants. The films on which the chapter focuses represent a range of efforts to render a fantastical and menacing Caribbean. These tropes of monstrosity pollinate several film genres (particularly horror and science fiction) and periods, but all the films are connected because they involve copious doses of the fantastic and are either set in the Caribbean or peopled by Caribbean characters. These films are discussed in three general groupings: pirate films, specifically the second and third installments of Disney's *Pirates of the Caribbean* series; the crime thrillers *Live and Let Die*, *Predator II*, *Marked for Death*, and *Bad Boys II*; and to a very limited extent, given the exhaustive work done on this genre, zombie films—*White Zombie*, *I Walked with a Zombie*, and *King of the Zombies*. The chapter is particularly interested in the way these films all tease to the fore the region's colonial legacy.

Chapter 3, "The Haunting of a Nation: Death and Discourse in Jamaica," considers allegedly factual reports of hauntings and other supernatural encounters that have gained national renown in Jamaica. Through these reports, the chapter explores questions of nationhood and identity by interrogating the narrative politics of stories about haunted locations and ghostly performances. This chapter, as well as chapter 4 and the conclusion, focuses on discourses about the fantastic generated in the region. The chapter asks, how do stories of spectral presences become well-known, nationally told tales that rise to the forefront of a nation's consciousness? And how do public discourses about supposedly real ghosts provide insight into a nation's imagination of itself at a specific historical moment? A few pan-Caribbean references to allegedly true reports of hauntings and other supernatural encounters are discussed, but the focus is on stories that have gained fame in Jamaica. These alleged hauntings, which took place in the twentieth century, include the story of the gruesome Kendall train crash tragedy from the mid-1950s, the sighting of three renegade crows piloting a casket in downtown Kingston, and the haunting of a Kingston community by a ghost known as Shirley.

Chapter 4, "Exodus: The Intergalactic Movement of Jah People in the Works of Tobias Buckell," explores futuristic representations of the region in Caribbean literature and contemplates how these literary acts of looking forward have been informed by the region's literary and experiential history.

The discussion begins with a theoretical discussion of the relationship between science fiction and the African diaspora, including the argument that slavery could be considered the original alien abduction tale—one is captured by strange creatures from another world, put on their ship, and taken away to a new geographic and cultural space in a world one did not even know existed. The chapter then offers a discussion about the advent of Afrofuturism before moving into an analysis of works by the contemporary Caribbean science fiction writer Tobias Buckell.

The book concludes with a short discussion of visual art from Caribbean artists, with an eye toward establishing how the deployment of the fantastic is reconceived in their work, and the appendix reproduces an interview with Buckell by the author.

CHAPTER ONE

British Obeah
The Making of Caribbean Savages

> Simply put, planters were attracted to Obeah because they
> could associate it with what they considered an un-Christian,
> residual Africanism and because they could readily connect
> it with death and destruction and radical irrationalism.
>
> SIMON GIKANDI

A surprising variety of British poems, novels, and plays produced during the eighteenth and nineteenth centuries involve references to the West Indies and the supernatural. Examples include Maria Edgeworth's story "The Grateful Negro"; Charlotte Smith Turner's novella *The Story of Henrietta*; "The Three Graves," a poem by Samuel Taylor Coleridge; "The Negro Incantation" by the Reverend William Shepherd; William Earle's novel *Obi; or, The History of Three-Fingered Jack*; and the British 1807 Christmas pantomime *Furibond; or, Harlequin Negro*. These works are either set in the West Indies or evoke the region, and all feature copious direct and indirect allusions to Caribbean magico-spiritual practices, including voodoo and Obeah. Most of this literature traffics heavily in these practices, depicting the region as unholy and uncivilized.

In contradiction to the way Obeah was often maligned in works such as these, Jerome Handler and Kenneth Bilby explain that it was a practice primarily aimed at facilitating wellness and justice in the slave community, addressing "socially beneficial goals such as healing, locating missing property, and protection against illness and other kinds of misfortune." Obeah was not entirely positive—it had "antisocial dimensions in the form of witchcraft or sorcery"—but according to Bilby and Handler, the "entirely negative view of Obeah that Whites largely promulgated during the period of slavery (probably exacerbated by the fact that it was sometimes directed against them), and that has endured until the present, has distorted the social role that Obeah played in the lives of many enslaved persons." Bilby and Handler add that whites denigrated Obeah by treating it as "a catch-all term for a range of supernatural-related ideas and behaviours that were not of European origin and which they heavily criticized and condemned."[1]

In his essay "Romantic Voodoo: Obeah and British Culture," Alan Richardson argues that in British texts featuring Obeah, it is persistently constructed as savage and primal, implying the inherent inferiority of Africans and assuaging Britain's national guilt over the tyranny of slavery. Furthermore, because these texts often did not situate Obeah in its appropriate historical context, the practice was represented as a "futile, empty gesture doomed to fail when met by European superiority," tacitly dispelling British fears of insurgency in the islands.[2] Scholars such as Richardson and Lizabeth Paravisini-Gebert, author of the essay "Colonial and Postcolonial Gothic: The Caribbean," have done substantial research on these British texts.[3]

I am particularly interested in the nonfiction texts produced by eighteenth- and nineteenth-century British writers attempting to document life in the West Indies. Caribbean-themed British literature from that era was heavily influenced by these voluminous historical publications, which include *The History of Jamaica* by Edward Long (1774), *The History, Civil and Commercial, of the British Colonies in the West Indies* by Bryan Edwards (1794), *Journal of a West India Proprietor* by Matthew "Monk" Lewis (1834), and *The English in the West Indies* by James Anthony Froude (1888). These books tried to describe, explain, and quantify the region and make it knowable within the boundaries of Europe's intellectual framework. Lewis, Edwards, Long, Froude, and other writers who sought to grapple with and define both blackness and the emerging colonized British spaces are important aspects of a critical consideration of literature from this period.

These nonfiction works offer extensive discussions of Obeah, often referred to as "Obi," and provide examples of people who were purportedly Obeahed; descriptions of Obi paraphernalia; and prolonged pontifications about how deluded the "negroes" were for believing any such thing could exist. Given the relationship between these texts' claims of conducting historical or ethnographic work and the creative products of the period, the questions that come to mind are how do these nonfiction texts define Obeah, and how do those definitions contribute to a more expansive effort to characterize blackness and the West Indies? British readers and theatergoers had long enjoyed ghost stories, and so, according to Diana Paton, "the depiction of people in the Caribbean as not only believers in the power of obeah but also as able to derive political force through this belief was a powerful sign of Caribbean difference to British audiences"—as well as "evidence of the depravity of Jamaican . . . culture."[4]

Long, Edwards, Lewis, and Froude share a generally similar narrative style. They present their writing as historically accurate, sometimes providing references, and statistical information as well as primary research. But the presumably academically sound posture these texts try to assume is undermined by their memoir-like characteristics and the perpetual interjection of a patronizing narrative voice that makes highly subjective proclamations about what it means to be black or West Indian. For example, Long's *The History of Jamaica* is laden with derisive commentary that helped animate the racist posture that came to define Europe's colonial venture. In one section of the text, Long describes blacks as inherently criminal: "In thieving they are thorough adepts, and perfectly accomplished. To set eyes on anything, and endeavour to possess it, is with them entirely the same."[5]

These writers situate Obeah as a malevolent, anti-intellectual undertaking laced with deceit. According to Long, Negroes "firmly believe in the apparition of specters," and "the most sensible among them fear the supernatural powers of the African *Obeah-men*." He repeatedly asserts the duplicity of Obeah practitioners through detailed descriptions of using plants to develop poisons and achieve some of the ostensibly magical effects attributed to the supernatural.[6] In *The History, Civil and Commercial, of the British Colonies in the West Indies*, Bryan Edwards condemns Obeah, which he defines as "a term of African origin, signifying sorcery or witchcraft, the prevalence of which, among many of their countrymen, all the Negroes most firmly and implicitly believe," as both naïve and savage.[7] Edwards includes extensive quotations from Long's work and heavily relies on it to inform his own writing, situating Long as an authority on the region. Matthew Lewis's *Journal of a West India Proprietor* reads as a somewhat more introspective account of life in the West Indies, but Lewis is overindulgent in his perpetual self-glorification, consisting of accounts of slaves and free blacks appealing to him for assistance or expressing their gratitude to him. But like Long and Edwards, Lewis denigrates Obeah and explains how he warned his slaves that he "should never hear the word Obeah, or any such nonsense mentioned on my estate, on pain of extreme displeasure."[8]

Froude offers a similarly antagonistic view of Obeah. He maligns the practice as cannibalistic and collapses Obeah and Vodun into one: "The African Obeah, the worship of serpents and trees and stones, after smouldering in all the West Indies in the form of witchcraft and poisoning, had broken out in Hayti in all its old hideousness. Children were sacrificed as in the old days of Moloch and were devoured with horrid ceremony, salted limbs being preserved and sold for the benefit of those who were unable to attend the full solemnities." Froude also yokes Haiti's alleged depravity to its independence by referring to Haiti with great disdain as "the republic of Toussaint l'Ouverture, the idol of all believers in the new gospel of liberty," and then commenting that "after ninety years of independence," it had "become a land where cannibalism could be practised with impunity."[9] Froude's juxtaposing of Haiti as epitomizing black independence and his wildly libelous claim of rampant cannibalism seeks to undermine the possibilities of successful black self-governance.

The attention paid to these practices was not without warrant, since a number of slave uprisings were closely associated with some enabling form of Afro-Caribbean spiritual practice. In Haiti, Makandal, the famed Vodun priest, or *houngan*, led a slave revolt in 1757.[10] As a *houngan*, Makandal's knowledge of the properties of particular plants would have facilitated the extensive use of poisons during the revolt.[11] A couple of decades later, the 1791 revolt was led by Boukman, another Vodun priest, who initiated the uprising with a nighttime Vodun ceremony.[12] During this ritual, the slaves' courage was bolstered by the promise of protection from the loas, the gods in the Vodun pantheon.[13] Boukman was born in Jamaica and taken to Saint-Domingue by a slave trader.[14] In the British West Indies, the traditions of Obeah and Myalism (a spiritual practice similar to Obeah) operated like Vodun and played key roles in several slave uprisings, including the 1760 Jamaican revolts led by a reputed Obeah man named Tacky.[15] Walter Rucker explains that when a fellow Obeah man and accomplice of Tacky's was captured, he "testified that he, along with his fellow practitioners, 'administered a powder, which being rubbed on their bodies, was to make them invulnerable.'"[16] Like Vodun, Obeah promised slave rebels protection, allowing them to envision the possibility of freedom and even sovereignty in the midst of severe oppression.[17]

Given the virulent antagonism shown toward Obeah in these texts, it is intriguing that the religion would play a significant thematic role in eighteenth- and nineteenth-century British literature. Obeah and other African-derived spiritual practices had a significant role in facilitating colonial Britain's shaping of ideas about Africa and blackness. Obeah is consistently represented in both nonfiction and fiction texts as an effete spiritual practice, hollow of substance and infused with the evil and treachery endemic to blackness. This British impulse to pathologize blackness underwrote the colonial imperative to define race. Dorothy Hammond and Alta Jablow suggest that the institution of the triangular trade coincided with this characterization of Africans as degenerate.[18] By exploiting the concept of race and using racial hierarchies to mark cognitive, cultural, and spiritual progress, or the lack thereof, European colonial powers were able to assert themselves as dominant and to vigorously infer the barbarity and deviance of colonized peoples.

Creating a Caribbean "Other"

Michel-Rolph Trouillot argues that the West has constructed history in ways that delegitimize the experiences of non-Europeans, who have been "treated as people without historicity," that is, without the ability to articulate accounts of their experiences. More specifically, he explains, Europeans are situated as having "claim to universal legitimacy" and that "the geography of imagination inherent in the West since the sixteenth century imposes a frame within which to read world history." Trouillot proposes that post-Columbian travel writers trafficked heavily in this notion of the Other and satisfied the European "demand for the Elsewhere" most often by filling what Trouillot terms the "the savage slot." This "slot" evolved because concurrent with the popularity of Enlightenment-era writing that featured fantastic geographies, like *Gulliver's Travels*, emerged the figure of the savage. Trouillot points out that "the savage or the primitive was the alter ego the West constructed for itself," but that alter ego was not unidimensional: "This Other was a Janus, of whom the Savage was only the second face." One face the West imagined as a utopia, the other as the bothersome savages inhabiting these utopian spaces.[19]

Analyses by other Caribbean studies scholars resemble Trouillot's and also propose the existence of some version of the "savage slot." Diana Paton and Maarit Forde argue that there has been tremendous reluctance to portray the region's pivotal role in the emergence of "modernity" and that "religion and ritual practice have largely been understood as antithetical to the modern."[20] In reference to W. E. B. Du Bois's notion of the "color line," Sylvia Wynter explains that black and brown people are the "ultimate conceptual Other," constructed in contrast to "the technological master of nature and ostensibly supracultural, autonomous 'Man' of the Western Bourgeoisie."[21] In Paget Henry's *Caliban's Reason: Introducing Afro-Caribbean Philosophy*, the author uses Shakespeare's *The Tempest* as a metaphor to demonstrate how the work of writers like Edwards and Long helped shape a European ideology that would in turn maintain colonial dominance: "Ideological machines had the biggest contracts with the political economy of Caribbean societies for producing the images and arguments that would sustain Prospero's dominance. As the dominant discourse, its practitioners were able to mobilize selected aspects of other discourses such as philosophy and history. To these appropriations they added large doses of racist dogma to produce the desired ideological outputs." Henry further explains that as part of conjuring an expedient European worldview that sustained the colonizers' foothold on power, Africans were situated as unable either to engage in "rational thought" or to gain that ability through training. The result, Henry avers, was a dissociation of colonizers from their "tribal" history and the reinvention of themselves as perpetually civilized.[22]

In his essay "The Economy of Manichean Allegory: The Function of Racial Difference in Colonialist Literature," Abdul JanMohamed crafts a theoretical framework for critically engaging with colonialist texts in ways that tease out this conspiratorial role in the establishment of racial difference. JanMohamed argues that colonialist literature's "fixation" on "the savagery and the evilness of the native should alert us to the real function of these texts: to justify imperial occupation and exploitation." According to JanMohamed, the ability of these texts to validate assumptions "that the barbarism of the native is irrevocable, or at least very deeply ingrained," authorized ongoing colonial interventions that involved taking advantage of the native's "resources," and facilitated, even encouraged assumptions of white "moral superiority." He further explains that the "Manichean allegory," which is the "central feature of the colonialist cognitive framework and . . . literary representation," consists of "a field of diverse yet interchangeable opposition between white and black, good and evil, superiority and inferiority, civilization and savagery, intelligence and emotion, rationality and sensuality."[23] JanMohamed more precisely defines his claim throughout the essay by developing a series of specific assertions.

He establishes a category of colonialist literature that he terms "imaginary" texts—works in which the "native functions as an image of the imperialist self." In these works, "indigenous people" are portrayed in ways that merge the "signifier with the signified," meaning that colonized people possess all the presumed characteristics of colonized spaces and are inherently barbaric and uncivilized. Specifically, "in the 'imaginary' colonialist realm, to say 'native' is automatically to say 'evil.'" This description situates as imaginary texts both the nonfiction and creative works that I analyze here. Such imaginary texts, according to JanMohamed, "fetishize" the Other and assume that the unsavory features associated with the colonized are not "products of social and cultural difference," but are instead markers of indelible racial variance. Furthermore, "the colonizer's invariable assumption about his moral superiority means that he will rarely question the validity of either his own or his society's formation and that he will not be inclined to expend any energy in understanding the worthless alterity of the colonized."[24]

Long, Edwards, Lewis, and Froude used their writing to do the work of establishing racial difference in the manner that JanMohamed suggests is representative of colonialist writing. While their texts comment on numerous aspects of black life in the New World, each writer wields Obeah as a particularly effective tool in their race-making arsenal. All of them try to situate Obeah as a practice embraced by all New World blacks, and this paves the way for them to easily fetishize the practice and use it as a symbolic representation of the entire race. Obeah is perhaps most prolifically used to establish the African's ignorance while simultaneously implying the European's intellectual superiority. Long writes, "In cases of poison, the natural effects of it are by the ignorant negroes, ascribed entirely to the potent workings of Obi" (Edwards 1794, 299).[25] Lewis refers to the "belief in Obeah" as "abominable," and cites Obeah as the cause for the intellectual and spiritual deficits of the slaves. He cites their non-Christian status (shown by their subscription to Obeah) and their consequent lack of belief in divine judgment as evidence of their moral corruption: "Their ignorance of a future state . . . makes them dread no punishment hereafter for themselves, and look with but little respect on human life in others."[26]

The perversity that propels Lewis's logic is revealed when he berates one of his slaves for believing that she has been Obeahed and "cursed," which was proved by her illness and the death of all her children. He tries to console her by giving her an abbreviated course in Christianity, explaining that God is "a great personage" who lives in the sky "in a place full of pleasures and free from pains" and that if she is "good," she will go to the sky and see her children again.[27] Lewis's intent in belittling the slave woman's belief in Obeah as primitive and anti-intellectual so consumes his focus that he is unable to recognize the irony in rejecting the woman's belief that a curse can cause a material effect and yet believing that a man lives in the sky along with the woman's dead children.

Obeah is further used to pathologize the black body through the persistent coupling of its practices with savagery. Edwards claims that when someone dies unexpectedly, New World blacks "never fail to impute it to the malicious contrivances and diabolical arts of some practitioner in *Obeah*." Their "funeral songs and ceremonies" are likewise disparaged as "nothing more than the dissonance of savage barbarity."[28] These funeral rites are described as "savage" because of their association with Obeah, which he portrays as a polluting agent that renders whatever it comes in contact with barbaric. Long similarly implies the subhuman status of blacks by animalizing Obeah practitioners, associating them with the body parts of animals: "Negroes wear the teeth of wild cats, and eat their flesh"; and he claims that they use items like fish bones and feathers as talismans.[29]

These early accounts of Obeah associate it with criminal behavior and depravity, too. Lewis narrates the story of entangled grievances between two of his slaves, Edward and Pickle. Pickle accused Edward of Obeahing him as well as of breaking into his house. Numerous similar instances occur throughout all four texts and involve someone being simultaneously accused of practicing Obeah and engaging in unlawful activity. In fact, practicing Obeah was made illegal in 1760. Obeah was also often associated with poisoning, and Long claims that this association is well documented: "The dexterity of these priests, or conjurers in the preparation of poisons, has been mentioned by many authors."[30] This recurrent casting of Obeah priests in the role of poison brewers further discredited the practice and suggested that it negatively informed moral choices.

These nonfiction writers explore other cultural practices and behaviors in dance, music, child care, sexuality, and hygiene, and they manipulate their commentary on these aspects of culture to establish the African's inferiority. Pathologizing slaves' belief in the supernatural, along with their sexuality, seems to have been particularly effective as a means of reifying racial difference. Europe's impulse to use the fantastic in the ways discussed here may have to do with its desired perception of itself as a society increasingly grounded in logic, seen most clearly in the Industrial Revolution. The fantastic certainly retreats from logic, and this perhaps explains its efficacy as a realm in which to establish difference and construct the African as anti-intellectual, morally corrupt, and barbaric.

An example of this construction is evident in William Earle's novella *Obi; or, The History of Three-Fingered Jack* (1800), a fictionalized account of the historic Jamaican figure known as Bristol, Jack Mansong, or Three-Fingered Jack. An article in a 1780 Jamaican newspaper identifies Three-Fingered Jack as the leader of a group of runaway slaves that allegedly terrorized a community known as Four Mile Wood by stealing food and supplies and attacking slaves. The article more specifically suggests that Jack and his posse were on a vendetta to "kill every Mulatto and Creole Negro they can catch." A bounty was placed on Jack by the Jamaican governor, and according to later reports, Jack was captured and killed by a Maroon named John Reeder. Pivotal to this story are the reports that emerges years later indicating Jack's affiliation with Obeah.[31]

Srinivas Aravamudan refers to the writings of the British physician Benjamin Moseley, who lived and worked in Jamaica for an extended time and claimed that Jack's possessions included "grave dirt," "the blood of a black cat," and "a dried toad." It is unclear how Moseley would have known the blood was from a cat, let alone that the cat was black. Aravamudan explains that "Moseley's account of Jack's final moments also mocks the Obeah elements, describing the failure of his imputed magical abilities and the triumph of his humbler adversaries through raw violence." Denigrating Obeah was, according to Aravamudan, a way to dismiss the rebels' motivations: "This focus on a mysterious religious practice shifts attention away from the political intentions and actions of slave rebels."[32]

Although *Obi* appears to be quite sympathetic to the plight of its antihero, Jack, it nonetheless diverts attention from the horror of slavery. The novella includes a backstory that reveals how Jack's parents were deceived and sold into slavery by a captain whose life they had saved. However, I would argue that the novel concomitantly repeats the slanders of writers such as Moseley, Lewis, Monk, Froude, and Edwards, who construct Obeah as a misshapen undertaking. In the novella, Jack is pathologized as vengeful, unable to assuage the hatred he feels for Europeans because of his devastating history. Furthermore, James Reeder, who kills Jack, had recently changed his name from Quashee and been christened. This rejection of his African heritage, signaled by his new name and by his choice to adopt a European religious practice, is shown to be Reeder's ultimate key to victory: "Reeder told him [Jack] Obi had no power over him, for that he was christened, and no longer Quashee, but James Reeder." This revelation overpowers his adversary: "Jack started back in dismay; he was cowed; for he had prophesied that White Obi should overcome him."[33] Jack, like a later fictional Jamaican gangster, Ivanhoe Martin, antihero of the classic cult film *The Harder They Come* (1972), lives shrouded in mystery and dies at the hands of the police—a force, like Reeder, affiliated with imperial power. Diana Paton argues that this portrayal of Jack as a bandit living on the margins of society is consistent throughout the numerous accounts of his story: "Jack is almost always a classic outlaw, reminiscent of older English outlaw heroes such as Robin Hood."[34] This depiction of Jack further associates Obeah and lawlessness.

Obeah and White Fears

European concerns regarding subversive activity like those attributed to Jack led to powerful anxieties about these practices. In fact, the situating of Afro-Caribbean religions as hollow and anti-intellectual stood in ironic contrast to evidence of the role played by these religions in acts of resistance throughout the Americas. Walter Rucker explains that these practices "served as conduits of powerful supernatural forces beyond the comprehension of their contemporaries and were, therefore, believed to be integral to the success of a number of slave resistance movements." The conjurers who claimed to wield these forces became "formidable and respected figures among enslaved Africans."[35] In fact, the work of Obeah practitioners posed a political threat in a number of Caribbean territories. Randy Browne argues that before Tacky's Rebellion, in 1760, "slaveholders and other European colonists largely ignored Obeah and saw African cultural practices as little more than evidence of Africans' supposed primitivism or heathenism." But after that revolt, Europeans began to view Obeah "with alarm and outlawed its practice throughout the West Indies, beginning with the 1760 Jamaican 'Act to Remedy the Evils Arising from Irregular Assemblies of Slaves.'" Violations of the law were severely punished: "Colonial courts routinely sentenced suspected Obeah practitioners to deportation or, in more extreme cases, execution." Similar laws aimed at curbing the practice of Obeah were passed in other parts of the Caribbean, including Guyana and Barbados. Despite these legal sanctions, the enslaved "continued to use Obeah despite."[36]

John Savage's work on Martinique reveals similar anxieties about Obeah. According to Savage, by the early nineteenth century, planters had become "obsessed with slave poisoning as a threat to the very 'survival of the island.'" Although this was not a new occurrence, reports sent to France indicated that the poisonings were becoming more vindictive and callous, involving harm to not only livestock and other slaves, but to white masters as well. The white plantocracy on Martinique came to believe these "poisonings were not the product of individual malefactors at all, but slaves who were controlled by a sophisticated network of African *obis*: sorcerers and 'black magicians' who had special knowledge of poison."[37] These suspicions about the practice of Obeah influenced how it and other Afro-Caribbean magico-religious pursuits were viewed by whites and how these practices were depicted in texts written by Europeans. Savage's explication of the plantocracy's reaction reinforces this project's contention that in many instances the colonial response to Afro-Caribbean religions unwittingly asserted their potency. The fear that these religions engendered was evidence of their potential to empower the enslaved, either because these supposedly futile practices could embolden them to take steps that would result in real destruction to the colonial enterprise, or because—and this was the more terrorizing possibility for Europeans—the practices actually worked.

Walter Rucker contends that throughout the New World, African-derived spiritual practices played an ongoing role in rebellions. A New York City slave revolt in 1712 was influenced by a figure known as Peter the Doctor. Rucker describes him as "a free African conjurer who rubbed a magical powder onto the clothing of the slaves to reportedly make them invulnerable." The fortified rebels, "armed with swords, knives, and guns[,] set fire to a building in downtown New York City and waited to ambush approaching Whites seeking to put out the blaze." The violence led by Peter the Doctor was not an isolated incident: "Conjurers and other African spiritualists were present in a variety of North American conspiracies and plots, including important examples in New York City in 1741, Richmond in 1800, and Charleston in 1822."[38]

In addition to their role in rebellions, Obeah practitioners were often considered effective healers, known for their expertise in curing a variety of ailments. Elsa Goveia reports a case from St. Kitts in 1789 that lauded the ability of practitioners who were sometimes able to treat and cure illnesses that "baffled" "regular" doctors. In fact, the agent writing the report noted his own successful treatment by Obeah practitioners.[39]

The Sociohistoric Context of British Writing about Obeah

To better understand the work of Long and the other writers under discussion, placing their work in a sociohistorical context is vital. Elsa Goveia astutely notes that Long diverted attention from the horrors of slavery: "[He] does not explain the character of the African by reference to his brutalization under the slave system. Instead he explains the brutality of the slave system by reference to the frightful character of Negroes." Long's writing, she maintains, commemorates "the power of all societies to mould, and often to warp, the minds and hearts of individuals that the social order may be preserved."[40] Goveia's comment is telling of the ways in which the historical moments that produced these works, and perhaps all works, influenced their character. A number of contemporary scholars expand on Goveia's claim and lay bare the social, political, and economic expediency associated with these representations and the strategic intentions that underlie fantastical constructions of the Caribbean. Most often, the effort seemed to be to displace the Caribbean from modernity and relieve Europe of any obligation to regard the region's non-European inhabitants as proper citizens worthy of the rights and liberties that the imperialist forces in the region assumed for themselves.

According to Diana Paton, for an extended portion of Caribbean history, Obeah functioned as "the ultimate signifier of the Caribbean's difference from Europe, a symbol of the region's supposed inability to be part of the modern world."[41] Like Goveia, Paton points out the hypocrisy inherent in the way Obeah became a target for the projection of European anxieties and a justification for the inhumanity of slavery: "Obeah in the Jamaicans' description became both a mirror to and an alibi for slavery and the slave trade. The lucrative and unjust trade under discussion becomes the one in 'Obies' rather than in human beings. Rather than slave-owners using their power and knowledge for exploitative purposes, it is Obeah men who do so. And rather than the system of slavery leading to the high mortality of the plantations, it is the slaves' belief in Obeah that is responsible."

Britain's major political concerns about the West Indies from the late eighteenth century to the late nineteenth, the period when works like those Goveia discusses were being published, provide a useful context for approaching these texts. In the late eighteenth century, one of the most pressing debates about the West Indies centered on the abolition of slavery. The publication dates of Long's, Edwards's, and Lewis's texts are bookended by relevant political milestones. In 1772, two years before Long's book appeared, Granville Sharp, chairman of the Committee to Abolish the Slave Trade, won a ruling in a case that prevented slave owners from forcibly sending their black servants from Britain to the West Indies to be sold into slavery; famously, the ruling stated that a slave became free when he set foot on English soil, since English law did not allow slavery. In 1833, the year before the publication of Lewis's text, the Abolition of Slavery Act was passed, bringing slavery gradually to an end throughout the British Empire. In the late nineteenth century, when Froude wrote, the debate about the region had shifted to encompass competing views on the feasibility of black sovereignty.

Simon Gikandi offers a cogent critique of the propensity to denigrate Obeah that is evident in the works of writers such as Long, Edwards, and Lewis. First, "Descriptions of Obeah and other forms of magic functioned in a fascinating dialectic of attraction and revulsion. Observers sought to represent the practice as a mark of black difference and to locate it in the realm of the irrational, which, in their mind defined the African." This representational practice constructed the African not only as removed from modernity, but also as barbaric and incapable of reason. Furthermore, Obeah and similar practices stoked white anxieties because, as Gikandi suggests, their locus of power was anchored in their inaccessibility to outsiders. For example, Gikandi makes this point in reference to Bryan Edwards: "What seemed to frustrate Edwards was not simply African delusions among the enslaved, but the inability of white proprietors to penetrate ritual codes of slaves and bring them under the regimen of modern knowledge." Gikandi adds that Myalism, an Afro-Caribbean spiritual practice anchored in dance, in fact created more anxiety for white planters than Obeah because "it was in Myalism that the African resistance to slavery was enshrined and an alternative set of beliefs cultivated." The keen focus and agitation surrounding Obeah was due to it being a more suitable and attractive target than Myalism for the dehumanizing of Africans.[42]

According to Gikandi, planters found value in Obeah because they viewed it as "an irrational Africanism": "Planters were attracted to Obeah because they could associate it with what they considered an un-Christian, residual Africanism and because they could readily connect it with death and destruction and radical irrationalism." But there was repulsion as well as attraction; Obeah provoked so much anxiety among colonizers that it was commonly punished by death or exile.[43] Diana Paton concurs that the obsession with Obeah was an effective strategy in the racializing of Africans: "Jamaicans' focus on Obeah, while a tactical error in the immediate and narrowly defined context of the debate about the slave trade, was in the longer term a valuable intervention on the side of the plantocracy." Paton goes on to explain that denigration of Obeah played a crucial role in the creating of black "savages" because it "helped to sustain a powerful image of black inferiority."[44]

Nana Wilson-Tagoe explains that the authors of the defamatory historical accounts discussed by Diana Paton were "often writing from the point of view of conquerors celebrating imperial glories and defending the validity of their social institutions." She contends that the production of Caribbean history has evolved in response to fluctuations in the region's dynamic "social" context, resulting in a "paradoxical perspective," a term that aptly describes the view of planter-historians who imposed European beliefs on the region in an effort to assess and define it. Wilson-Tagoe cites the historian Elsa Goveia's comment, "In the writing of West Indian history the most potent atmosphere underlying interpretation have often been drawn from outside the subject," and further identifies the "irony" that an "array of distinctly local material should have been analyzed and judged not in terms of the region's particularity and future but by ideas and beliefs developed in the context of other societies and other futures."[45]

Wilson-Tagoe clarifies that the approach to historical methodology used by writers such as Long and Edwards was "based on description and analysis as a supplement to the narration of events." In particular, Long's historical account "was inspired by a belief in the possibility of an internally autonomous Jamaica." And while his perspective offered a "radical and revolutionary view of what Jamaica could become," he accommodated his racism by believing that his "liberal" views were not applicable to the enslaved. Wilson-Tagoe describes Long's approach to historiography as a "failure of historical interpretation," and this assessment seems equally applicable to the work of Edwards and the other writers discussed in this chapter. Wilson-Tagoe identifies Edwards's writing as being rooted in what she describes as "a 'Creole' defense against the English humanitarians and abolitionists." His book downplayed the genocide of Africans and indigenous populations as "a Christian country's defeat of a savage people."[46] Paton agrees with that assessment, calling Edwards's book "a formative pro-slavery and white creole work which sought to demonstrate the value of the colonies and the legitimacy of slavery, against increasingly influential abolitionism." Paton further contends that "the widespread urge on the part of Britons and Anglo-Caribbean people to tell stories about Obeah," particularly "in their emphasis on the occult power of enslaved people[,] . . . displaced an anxiety into an argument about racial hierarchy."[47]

Froude aimed to affirm this racial hierarchy in *The English in the West Indies* (1888). It was published when an uneasy dialogue about the possibility of black sovereignty was emerging in Britain, much to the trepidation of some. A conversation between Froude's text and this dialogue clearly took place. Faith Smith makes this point forcefully: "It would be absurd to deny the impact a text such as *The English in the West Indies* had on British colonial policy, as well as its contribution to the prevailing metropolitan image of a Caribbean inhabited by lazy Negroes and a well-meaning but beleaguered plantocracy."[48] This conversation was an aspect of a larger idea: "Intellectual formation in nineteenth century Britain cannot be fully understood outside of the context of the relationship between Britain and the rest of the world." Froude's work and his unabashed defamatory remarks about the region helped create an intellectual framework for reinforcing notions of white racial superiority and the unfeasibility of black sovereignty in Britain's colonies.

Other critics share Smith's perception of the political interplay between Britain and its colonies. Lara Putnam claims that constructions of religious practices in the Caribbean like those seen in texts such as Froude's and Spenser St. John's *Hayti: The Black Republic* "became key evidence for those debating ex-slaves' readiness for political rights."[49] Additionally, Wilson Harris ascribes Froude's political posture to his distaste for change: "Froude distrusted change since in his estimation everything was so dicey, so fortuitously consolidated that change, in fact was likely to rob it of any conservative historical shape it already possessed."[50]

Nana Wilson-Tagoe likewise argues that Froude "conceived of history as progress and development," "as the quickening and growth of human physical and intellectual energy in an atmosphere of the rule of the strong over the weak." This quickening and growth occurred "not in the freedom in which the modern society takes delight, but under the sharp rule of the strong over the weak." In fact, Wilson-Tagoe describes Froude's writing as a "proslavery argument."[51]

Caribbean studies scholars including Goveia, Paton, Wilson-Tagoe, Smith, and Gikandi acknowledge and illuminate the strategically defamatory work of the writers discussed in this chapter. Their writings provide a rich and telling example of some of Europe's earliest efforts to use the Caribbean fantastic in the racializing of the region. What is more, these portrayals do the labor of pathologizing the Caribbean and distracting attention from the ravaging effects of slavery and the colonial project.

CHAPTER TWO

Devilish Divas and Gangster Monsters

*Hollywood's Monstrous
Imaginings of the Caribbean*

> We always knew that the dismantling of the colonial paradigm would release strange demons from the deep, and that these monsters might come trailing all sorts of subterranean material.
>
> STUART HALL

This chapter is concerned with Hollywood's representation of the Caribbean in film—specifically, films that feature a fantastical element. These films often depict an enchanted Caribbean capable of seducing outsiders into abandoning sound judgment or enabling insiders to engage in horrifying undertakings. Teeming with supernatural entities, the Caribbean of Hollywood's imagination as portrayed in these films is destructive, seductive, and laden with monsters. The region, or its symbolic representative, is usually situated as a powerful but deadly lure. The films discussed here were made by Hollywood and represent a range of efforts to render a fantastical and menacing Caribbean. The specific genres of the films (horror, sci-fi, and so forth) are less important than the fact that they provide copious doses of the fantastic and are set in the Caribbean or peopled by Caribbean characters. I am intrigued by Hollywood's commentary on the region, especially since the Caribbean's own literature, music, and film productions have been significantly influenced by Hollywood. In a space where the eyes of its inhabitants voraciously consume an infinite number of moving images created outside the region, how do the creators of those images, which have in some ways transfixed the region's gaze, gaze back on the Caribbean?

To lend some coherence to my discussion, I explore these films in three groupings, starting with the second and third installments of Disney's *Pirates of the Caribbean* series. Next, I offer a brief discussion of the zombie films *White Zombie*, *I Walked with a Zombie*, and *King of the Zombies*. While a significant amount of critical discourse already exists about this genre, the early zombie films in particular are fundamental to any discussion of the portrayal of the region in film and provide a useful historical context for my discussion of contemporary films. Last, I explore crime thrillers—*Live and Let Die*, *Predator II*, *Marked for Death*, and *Bad Boys II*. All these films tease to the fore the region's history of imperialism while revealing some of the complex identities that have emerged on the screen in the last century in relation to the region, often defying the usually anticipated binaries.

For example, pirates, the quintessential popular-culture icons associated with the Caribbean, reveal the antagonisms that nourished Europe's colonial project in the region. Nevertheless, in the *Pirates of the Caribbean* franchise, Johnny Depp's satirical portrayal of Captain Jack Sparrow as both a dandy and a hypermasculine buccaneer, as both white and black (implied through, among other things, his dreadlocks), interferes with the inclination to read Depp's characterization of Sparrow as anything but a hybrid subject. Similar attention to nuance is required in a discussion of "gangster monsters"— the monstrous black villains in the crime thrillers discussed here. They are characterized as monstrous in both action and appearance, and they are racialized. Despite the troubling depiction of these villains in ways that imply their impotency against the militarized police forces associated with white metropolitan centers, most of the "gangster monsters" are defeated with the aid of African American subjects.

Furthermore, all the films racialize the Caribbean, contributing to its characterization as marginalized. According to Sidney Mintz, the region's legacy of slavery "blackened" and "Africanized" the Caribbean, resulting in cultures heavily influenced by Africa.[1] In *Otherness in Hollywood Cinema*, Michael Richardson makes a somewhat related claim about how geographic location influences the characterization of specific locales in films. He contends that Hollywood implies the "otherness" of the Deep South and the Midwest by making them the settings for horror movies, while most other films are set in only a few metropolitan cities.[2] With Richardson's claim in mind, the Hollywood imaginary seems to envision the Caribbean as a similarly fecund setting for the unfolding of the fantastic, given the region's "blackened" identity.

The concept of abjection, often associated with the work of Julia Kristeva, is useful for this discussion. Kristeva defines the abject in numerous ways: "What disturbs identity, system, order. What does not respect borders, positions, rules. The in-between, the ambiguous, the composite."[3] The films discussed here construct the Caribbean as a repository for the abject, a venue inhabited by the marginalized and unwanted, those who do not properly dwell within the desirable boundaries inscribed by Eurocentric ideals. In *The Inhuman Race*, Leonard Cassuto identifies this concept of the abject with the "grotesque," which, he argues, "has a peculiar disruptive power—it is a conflicting mixture of signals that intrudes upon the desired order of the world," adding, "tension is the common element to virtually every definition of the term."[4] In the films I discuss, that abjection and grotesqueness is transposed into the monstrous as orders of sorcerers, ghouls, and zombies. These beings express their peripheral status as racialized others via the grotesque and transgressive nature of their monstrous embodiment.

One important question to consider is where does the gaze ascribing monsterhood originate in the ideological terrain? (I am using Laura Mulvey's concept of the gaze put forward in her essay "Visual Pleasure and Narrative Cinema.")[5] I believe some elements of the characterization of these monsters meant to signify transgression and unruliness are not read by people who reside in or are affiliated with marginalized groups as a trespass into inappropriate territory. For example, in many non-European cultures, the ability of people to possess alternate epistemological capabilities—different ways of gaining knowledge—is quite acceptable, and people with powers akin to, say, those of Tia Dalma, the sorceress in *Pirates of the Caribbean*, are often revered as an important part of the community.

Scholars have theorized about the link between fantastical portrayals like that of Tia Dalma and the European colonial project. For example, Joan Dayan proposes that there is an intimate connection between the atrocities of the colonial experience in the Caribbean and the fantastic: "I am suggesting that we connect remembered torture with oppressive magic. Phantoms of domination and scenes of the past return, transmogrified and reinvested with new meanings."[6] Dayan asserts this analysis specifically in reference to the relationship between Caribbean myths about creatures who shed their skin and the cruel punishment of slaves in Saint-Domingue, who were whipped until their skin lifted to expose their flesh, and then had substances such as salt and pepper applied to their open wounds in an egregious act of torture.

Bliss Cua Lim, too, proposes a link between colonialism and fantastic cinema: "Imperialist discourse depended on a temporal strategy in which radical cultural differences brought to light by colonial contact were framed as primitive and anachronistic." Lim argues that "imperialist discourse" employed mechanisms that involved a kind of gerrymandering of temporal boundaries, and he cites Anne McClintock, who argues that "colonized people—like women and the working class in the metropolis—do not inhabit history proper but exist in a permanently anterior time within the geographic space of the modern empire." Lim seems to suggest that "fantastic cinema" furnishes opportunities for a "temporal critique" that would ultimately implicate colonialism.[7]

While Lim and other scholars such as Istvan Csicsery-Ronay and John Rieder analyze how colonialism has informed fantastic genres, other theorists, such as Ed Guerrero, Adilifu Nama, and Isiah Lavender III, recognize the implicit connections between race (and, inevitably, slavery and colonialism) and the fantastic. For example, Guerrero asserts that in film, "the social construction and representation of race, *otherness*, and non-whiteness is an ongoing process, working itself out in many symbolic, cinematic forms of expression, but particularly in the abundant racialized metaphors and allegories of the fantasy, sci-fi, and horror genres."[8] Nama similarly finds the fantastic to be fertile ground for probing race, even when black representation is negligible. Nama argues that "in spite of the overt omission of black representation and racial issues in SF cinema, . . . both are present in numerous SF films."[9]

Some of these critical frameworks have been proposed for discussing specific genres of the fantastic (faint as these genre boundaries often are) or specific types of creative products (such as literature or film). While I do not present an exhaustive list of theoretical approaches relevant to critiquing films that construct a fantastical Caribbean, the approaches I mention represent ideas from a range of thinkers on the subject of race and fantasy. For me, these approaches are most useful because they acknowledge an intimate bond between race and fantasy and suggest that the fantastic is a venue for working through the colonial experience and its resultant anxieties and conflicts, as well as its by-product of racial trauma.

I rely most substantively on the work of Joshua Bellin. In *Framing Monsters: Fantasy Film and Social Alienation*, Bellin argues that "there is a long-standing (and ongoing) tradition in fantasy film that identifies marginalized social groups as monstrous threats to the dominant social order." Bellin also addresses the potentially alienating effects of the genre: "Because fantasy films can activate audience prejudices while preventing audiences from recognizing" or "taking responsibility for such prejudices, they are ideal agents of social alienation: their seeming purity permits their pollution." This chapter pursues and interrogates how Caribbean "monsters" are framed by the movie camera and what those framing strategies seem to suggest about the region and its inhabitants. Bellin believes that fantasy films engage in the project of "stigmatizing or scapegoating" those with limited power, who are "made to bear disproportionate responsibility for social anxieties and ills."[10]

Chet Van Duzer explains that foreign landscapes have long been associated with monsters: "Since the ancient Greek period, what were perceived by Europeans to be the distant edges of the earth have been thought to be the realm of exotica—of treasures, strange animals, and monstrous beings."[11] Additionally, in "The Monstrous Caribbean," Persephone Braham suggests, like Bellin, that monstrosity operates on a representational level as a stand-in for the abject: "Embodying exoticism, hybridity, and excess, monsters sustained the ongoing conceptualization of the unknown that was a prerequisite to conquest and colonization; after independence, monsters became metaphors for a series of problems ranging from indigenous and African slavery to dictatorship and postcolonial identity."[12] Bellin further argues that the way these monsters are constructed suggests that whatever torture or abuse they experience, they presumably warrant, or even desire. These films thus expose, in Bellin's words, "deeply rooted yet largely unarticulated cultural beliefs" and "serve to focus, quicken, and vindicate energies of contempt, suspicion, rage, and violence against the vulnerable and disempowered." Bellin's ideas are informed by the work of René Girard, and a quotation from Girard provides the epigraph for Bellin's introduction: "Monstrosity actualizes the tendency of all persecutors to project the monstrous results of some calamity or public or private misfortune onto some poor unfortunate who, by being infirm or a foreigner, suggests a certain affinity to the monstrous. Instead of bearing certain faintly monstrous characteristics, the victim is hard to recognize as a victim because he is totally monstrous."[13]

Girard's concept of the scapegoat, advanced in his book of the same name, suggests that vilifying certain groups or their symbolic representatives, including religious and racial minorities as well as outsiders and the mentally unstable, and making them into monsters obscures our ability to recognize someone who has been persecuted, because their horrifying characteristics deflect our attention. Guerrero conceives of monsters similarly: "The 'monster' always constitutes the return of the socially or politically repressed fears of a society, those energies, memories, and issues that a society refuses to deal openly with."[14] The disempowerment often associated with these types of "monsters" is also associated with black and brown people. Given that the Caribbean is populated by and also affiliated with these racial minority groups, the region has become a rich source of the ghouls who people fantastical films. This chapter proposes approaches for unmasking these ghoulish figures by reassociating them with the group that inspired their creation in the first place.[15] To borrow Lavender's term, I intend to interrogate and expose the "blackground," that is, "the embedded perceptions of race and racism," in the films I survey, with a particular eye toward how they racialize the Caribbean.[16] John Rieder suggests that in relation to science fiction, "the exotic, once it had been scrutinized, analyzed, theorized, catalogued, and displayed, showed a tendency to turn back upon and re-evaluate those who had thus appropriated and appraised it."[17] Here I intend to reevaluate the monstrous on behalf of the Caribbean, particularly to uncover how the fantastic has been appropriated in speculative genres featuring the Caribbean and thereby to expose the anxieties that nurture hegemonic relationships with the region.

It should first be pointed out that Hollywood has had a lengthy and sometimes vexed relationship with the Caribbean. Well before the advent of U.S. cable television stations and a deluge of other foreign media, which are sometimes implicated as the cause of a variety of problems in the region, there was the cinema, an institution that has historically had a critical role in the shaping of Caribbean culture. In the Anglophone Caribbean, this influence is apparent in a number of cultural artifacts. One of the most popularly critiqued aspects of this influence is the Caribbean's romance with the gun-slinging cowboy western, an aesthetic evident in Caribbean films like *The Harder They Come* and *Shottas* (2002), in which scenes unfold that mimic classic stylistic elements of the western genre. Furthermore, books such as V. S. Naipaul's *A House for Mr. Biswas* (1961) and his linked-story collection *Miguel Street* (1959), Earl Lovelace's novel *The Dragon Can't Dance*, and Michael Thelwell's novel *The Harder They Come* (1980) feature characters whose identities are collapsed into that of movie characters. Some of these texts comment on the impact of Hollywood on fictional communities. For example, the narrator of *Miguel Street* explains of one character: "It was something of a mystery why he was called Bogart; but I suspect that it was Hat who gave him the name. I don't know if you remember the year the film Casablanca was made. That was the year when Bogart's fame spread like fire though Port of Spain and hundreds of young men began adopting the hard boiled Bogartian attitude."[18] These literary characters then become analogues of film characters. Despite profound differences of race, class, and culture, Caribbean audiences have historically had no difficulty with this merger of their personae with mostly white, wealthy, American performers. Keith Warner states explicitly that black audiences in the Caribbean "saw no incongruity in identifying with white actors and what they were portraying."[19]

The cinema's influence on Caribbean culture is also evident in the region's music and its accompanying performance events. As early as in the 1940s, Trinidadian carnival bands began adopting movie-inspired names such as Casablanca and Destination Tokyo. Sailor costumes increased in popularity not only because of the American naval base in Trinidad but also because of the numerous war films depicting the military. Warner explains that calypso and soca music expose this embrace between Hollywood and Caribbean culture in songs such as Mighty Sparrow's "Gunslingers" that refer to specific films or Hollywood names. Furthermore, some reggae and dancehall performers have assumed stage names influenced by Hollywood, such as Charlie Chaplin and Dennis Alcapone.[20] Songs such as Desmond

Dekker's "007 Shanty Town" invoke Hollywood via film references, in this instance to the 1960 film *Ocean's 11*, starring, among others, Frank Sinatra and Sammy Davis Jr. Dekker sings:

> 0-0-7
> At ocean eleven
> and the rudeboys a go wail,
> 'Cause them out of jail,
> Rudeboys cannot fail,
> 'Cause them must get bail[21]

Just like the novels mentioned earlier, Dekker's song intertwines a Caribbean identity, the "rude boy," with that of the similarly disorderly characters in *Ocean's 11*, a sort of lyrical identity merger.

The Caribbean's reliance on Hollywood as a source of inspiration for its cultural products contains an intriguing irony. Whereas Hollywood's vision of the region often energizes the region's vision of itself, in some instances it is capitalized upon by Caribbean subjects for financial and other benefits. An example is the use of the increasingly popular ghost-tourism model for the marketing of the Rose Hall great house in Jamaica. The home page for this popular tourist destination advertises the "Rose Hall Great House Haunted Night Tour," which draws on the location's historical association with hauntings.[22]

Pirates of the Caribbean

The *Pirates of the Caribbean* series is inspired by the Disney theme park ride after which the films are named, and like the Rose Hall legend, the series invokes its own fictionalized legends. The series stars the contemporary Hollywood "rude boy" Johnny Depp. The second and third installments, *Pirates of the Caribbean: Dead Man's Chest* (2006) and *Pirates of the Caribbean: At World's End* (2007), each grossed roughly $1 billion worldwide.[23] Directed by Gore Verbinski, produced by Jerry Bruckheimer, and starring Depp as the iconic Captain Jack Sparrow, this fantasy series catapults audiences into Sparrow's eighteenth-century world of magical adventure on the high seas of the Caribbean and beyond. The films, especially *Dead Man's Chest* and *At*

World's End, are steeped in the fantastic and feature, among numerous other mythical elements, a magical compass, a crew of monstrous "undead" pirates, and a sorceress named Tia Dalma.

The series gestures toward predecessors such as *The Black Pirate* (1926), *Captain Blood* (1935), and *The Buccaneer* (1958), but with a wink and a dandified nod that announce the series' self-awareness and its pervasive mockery of the genre from which it derives. Of the films' send-up of genre conventions, the most irreverent one, and the one most amusing in its subterfuge, is Depp's portrayal of Sparrow. Both cowardly and brave, villainous and heroic, hypermasculine and effeminate, Sparrow sashays through the series with heavily lined eyes and the gait of a fashion model while dexterously wielding his sword and mercilessly dispatching his enemies. Depp's complex portrayal of Sparrow is enhanced by his dreadlocks, which are often associated with the Caribbean, reggae icons like Bob Marley, and the religious practice of Rastafarianism. Margarite Olmos and Lizabeth Paravasini-Gebert describe Rastafarianism as "a twentieth century religious and political phenomenon that originated in Jamaica and has gained international attention as a Pan-African approach to the problems of poverty, alienation, and spirituality." Rastafarianism was founded on Christian principles and disavows "magicoreligious practices such as Obeah."[24] The culturally associated hair aesthetic of dreadlocks has become a potent signifier of cultural resistance.[25]

While Sparrow's locks gesture toward his marginalized position as part of a counterculture, they also invoke the racist anxieties that dreadlocks and their associations with blackness, violence, and lawlessness have spawned in the Hollywood imaginary.[26] Numerous aspects of Depp's portrayal of Sparrow, along with other subversive elements in the films, were not authorized by Disney. Anne Peterson suggests that the series was "pirated," its original trajectory pried away by Depp, Verbinski, and the writers, who, she contends, added "character ambiguity, a troubled story arc, anti-heroes, and off-color humor to the traditionally chaste Disney text."[27] In an interview with Patti Smith for *Vanity Fair*, Depp commented that the Disney establishment "couldn't stand" his portrayal of Sparrow and that the then head of Disney, Michael Eisner, accused him of "ruining the movie."[28] Sparrow's unruliness bears an uncanny resemblance to the lawlessness associated with historical Caribbean piracy and has an even more uncanny connection with the contemporary personae of black Caribbean gangsters, or rude boys.

Historically, pirates, like slaves and native Amerindians, existed on the margins of eighteenth-century Caribbean culture. In her thoughtfully conceived essay "Welcome the Outlaw: Pirates, Maroons, and Caribbean Countercultures," Erin Mackie explains that the composition of pirate crews included indentured workers who had absconded from their employment, criminals, and poor white men unable to compete in the Caribbean's labor market, where free labor was violently secured from slaves and natives.[29] According to Sidney Mintz, "for most of the islands during most of their post-Columbian history, labor had to be impressed, coerced, dragged, and driven to work."[30] So the social status of the kind of men who often became pirates, regardless of their race, certainly bore a relationship to the marginalized status of slaves. Furthermore, piracy and seamanship in general became a pathway to freedom for many black men in the Americas. W. Jeffrey Bolster explains that black men "joined disgruntled white soldiers, sailors, and servants confederating as pirates along sun-drenched Caribbean sea-lanes," where they managed to develop "an egalitarian, if ephemeral, social order that rejected imperial society's hierarchy and forced labor."[31] The dreadlocks worn by many of the pirates in the *Pirates of the Caribbean* films, their often sooty faces, and the preponderance of black shipmates inscribe their metaphorical blackness and facilitate the symbolic representation of their subcultural identity. In fact, Hollywood has historically conceived of pirates as a marginalized population, and the 1926 silent film *The Black Pirate*, starring Douglas Fairbanks, featured a black shipmate during an era when very few films had an integrated cast.

Erin Mackie illuminates the marginalized status of pirates when she explains that the pirate, rude boy, Rastafari, and Maroon subcultures reside in similar territory and are "vital embodiments of historical complicity." She argues that their "outlaw" status unites them as Caribbean countercultures. Furthermore, she implies that the modern figure of the rude boy is the heir apparent to the historical figure of the Caribbean pirate.[32] In a speech during the famed One Love Peace Concert, held in Kingston in 1978, Peter Tosh (formerly of the Wailers) perceptively commented on the Caribbean's lineage of violence. The concert was held to observe a peace treaty between warring political factions, and according to Sebastian Clarke, Tosh "saw the whole operation as futile" and believed that "true peace could only be obtained by improving the material condition of the urban poor."[33] Tosh demystified the roots of the violence plaguing the nation by fusing the region's historical legacy of outlaw pirates and the contemporary advent of outlaw rude boys:

> Members of Parliament must come together to deal with poor people and the suffering class and the police to know that they brutalize poor people, an fe what? . . . When Columbus, Henry Morgan and Francis Drake come up, dey call dem pirate and put them in a reading book and give us observation that we must look up and live the life and the principle of pirates. So the youth dem know fe fire dem guns like Henry Morgan same way . . . Is just a shitstem lay down to belittle the poor.[34]

In a move similar to that made by Tosh in his commentary, Depp's portrayal of Sparrow collapses piracy, in its historic context as a counterculture, into its descendant the contemporary rude boy, an identification implied by Sparrow's dreadlocks. Sparrow's complexity is further heightened because he simultaneously occupies the space of ancestor, as a European, and of offspring, based on his blackened identity (implied by his locks), occupation, and romantic history with a black woman. Given piracy's rebellious legacy as well as Depp's proclivity for resisting convention, it is no surprise then that Tia Dalma, a black woman and Obeah or Vodun priestess, emerges as Sparrow's former love interest and ally.

Tia Dalma, who is featured in the second and third installments of the series, is shrouded in magic and mystery. She lives in the remote interior of a creepy swamp, her home a sinister-looking tree house filled with magical accoutrements. She is highly sexualized and flirtatious from her first appearance on-screen, when Sparrow and some of his crew go to seek her help in *Dead Man's Chest*. Furthermore, her sexual dalliances with the sea captain Davy Jones and her subsequent betrayal of him are at the heart of the plot in the film. Tia Dalma's portrayal reflects in some ways the characteristics associated with Erzulie Freda (or Ezili), a loa in the Haitian Vodun pantheon who is "usually compared to Aphrodite" and "belongs to the family of sea spirits." She is also described as "coquettish, sensual, pleasure-loving, and extravagant," her life "a succession of scandals" because of her liaisons with other loas, some of whose advances she indifferently rejects.[35] Tia Dalma's Erzulie-esque characteristics collaborate to render her (and by implication the Caribbean) as enchanted and alluring, but also as dangerous and capable of causing severest heartbreak.

Tia Dalma is first seen during Sparrow's terrifying but urgent trek to solicit her help with getting information about a key. Before that, Sparrow intimates his anxiety over her seductive powers. As he and his crew approach her home in the swamp, he suggests that he and Tia Dalma have a romantic history, and in a rare display of uncertainty and hesitation, he expresses his apprehension as he tries to define their prior liaisons. "Don't worry, mates," he assures his crew as they meander through the fog-shrouded swamp and approach her eerie tree house, "Tia Dalma and I go way back. Thick as thieves. Nigh, inseparable we are." Then he hesitates as he tries to redefine their relationship with more temporal accuracy: "Were," he says then pauses. "Have been," he murmurs, looking a bit puzzled, then pauses again. "Before," he finally adds quizzically, appearing confused. Sensing his hesitation, one of the crew members assures Sparrow that they will "watch his back." But Sparrow very tellingly replies, "It's me front I'm worried about," alluding to Tia Dalma's persistent potency as a seductress to whose wiles Sparrow remains subject.

Tia Dalma does in fact possess a kind of dominion over masculine energies. Her power is inscribed in the scene when Jack first arrives at her home. He peeps in through glass panes in the front door, crouching and timidly peering in; Tia Dalma's dominance is palpable. The house is bedecked with numerous bottles hanging from the tree limbs that structure her ceiling. These dangling bottles, thought to ward off evil spirits, are a common feature of Obeah.[36] Furthermore, Tia Dalma is versed in the Yoruban divination practice of Ifá, the casting and then interpretation of collections of objects to reveal information. In a later scene, she casts a handful of crab claws to identify the location of Davy Jones's ship. Supernatural and religious undertones are further evinced by clusters of candles burning throughout the house, casting an eerie glow while suggesting religious altars. Additionally, a menacing snake is loitering in a branch at her doorway, bringing to mind the Garden of Eden and the threat of impending temptation as well as the presence of evil. After Jack hesitantly enters Tia Dalma's house, we finally see her, and her long and unruly dreadlocks frame her face and evoke Medusa's slithering head of snakes.

When Sparrow leaves Tia Dalma, he is satisfied with the outcome of his visit. But by the close of the movie, Sparrow has a new set of troubles: he and his ship have been dragged into the sea by the kraken, Davy Jones's sea monster. *Dead Man's Chest* closes with Sparrow's crew and comrades returning to Tia Dalma for refuge. As they make their way back to see her, they notice that the inlet leading to her house is lined with black people holding candles. Their bodies are halfway immersed in the murky water, a distortion of the traditional baptismal ritual. These ghostly figures stand in silence, their faces sallow and grim as they stare at the crew, seemingly mourning the crew's loss as well as their own. These spectral figures in ragged clothing who reside in the swamp with Tia Dalma could be the spirits of slaves, immobilized by the trauma of slavery: they barely move, and they don't speak. The construction of this scene suggests that Tia Dalma functions as an archive of Caribbean memory.

Kameelah Samuel suggests that the people lining the inlet are Maroons, living under Tia Dalma's guardianship.[37] This very literal reading of their presence does not compete with the possibility that their ghostly features position them as being just as otherworldly as Tia Dalma. Whether human or something in between, they are certainly engaged in a form of marronage that displaces them from both the seat of colonial rule and a dense form of physical embodiment. Additionally, their way of clustering around Tia Dalma's home implies that aside from her being an archive of Caribbean memory, she is a repository of the region's pain and a receptacle for Caribbean history.

Tia Dalma ends up consoling Sparrow's crew and promises to lead them on a journey to rescue Sparrow from the underworld. *At World's End*, the next film in the series, begins with that rescue mission. Tia Dalma has joined Sparrow's crew and repeatedly uses her magical powers to help guide the crew to Sparrow. During the course of the film, we come to understand that Tia Dalma is in fact the sea goddess Calypso, bound in human form—a lynchpin in the film's plot and the cause for Davy Jones's monstrous embodiment. She ends up striking a deal with Captain Barbossa, a pirate whom she brought back to life, to release her from her bondage in human form. She is brought on deck and bound neck to feet in rope, and then Barbossa performs the ritual to release her. Initially, she grows into a giant version of herself, towering several stories above the ship, and then she explodes into a landslide of crabs that crawl into the ocean, and finally she resumes her identity as a sea goddess, literally immersing herself in the Caribbean Sea, embodying the region's identity. The low-angle shots of Tia Dalma after she becomes a monster help emphasize her monstrosity, but in an ironic twist, these images takes on religious undertones and includes the mast of the ship, which forms a cross behind her, further suggesting her status as a divine but persecuted entity.

Tia Dalma's function as a symbolic embodiment of the Caribbean is energized by components of her persona that are inflected with a Caribbean identity. Among the most immediately apparent is her speech. Unlike the other characters in the series, most of whom, quite curiously, do not have Caribbean accents, hers is very pronounced—an eighteenth-century Miss Cleo, if you will. Given the historical dearth of roles for black women in Hollywood, it is noteworthy that Tia Dalma was cast as a black woman and that Naomie Harris, who plays her, is of Caribbean heritage.[38] The selection of Harris for this role suggests that Disney was quite keen on having Tia Dalma's character be black and identifiable as Caribbean. The casting of Harris is particularly meaningful because the films in some ways erase traces of a black Caribbean presence, which at that time would have consisted primarily of slaves, and instead prominently feature blacks as members of pirate crews. This erasure is particularly evident in the opening film of the series, *The Curse of the Black Pearl*, in which all the servants in the governor's mansion are, quite peculiarly, white. Kevin Frank argues that this is a result of Disney's "utopian" impulse and its unwillingness to represent the reality of the region's black and enslaved population.[39] Tia Dalma's Caribbean-ness is further inscribed by her hair, which, like Sparrow's and Dave Jones's, is dreadlocked. Additionally, her face is adorned with a design that approximates tribal scarification, linking her with the region's African slaves and indigenous peoples. According to Kameelah Samuel, "before Tia Dalma steps into the frame, the audience is already queued [*sic*; cued] as to how to read her character—scary, otherworldly, and sexually aggressive."[40] Tia Dalma's symbolic function as the Caribbean is also implied by her association with elements of African-derived spiritual practices such as Obeah.

Tia Dalma's secret identity as the Greek goddess Calypso offers another useful analytical approach for relating Tia Dalma to the Caribbean. Calypso was a nymph, perhaps best known from Homer's *Odyssey*. Calypso seduces

Odysseus when he is shipwrecked on her island, imploring him to become her husband and promising him eternal youth. She holds him captive for seven years, until the gods intervene to secure his release. Odysseus describes Calypso as a "dread goddess" with "ordered hair," adding, "there is no one, neither a god nor mortal person, / who keeps her company." During Odysseus's stay with her, he claims, "[She] loved me excessively and cared for me, and she promised to make me an immortal and all my days to be ageless." But Odysseus is forlorn, persistently "drenching with tears that clothing, immortal stuff, Kalypso had given."[41] His assessment of Calypso's physical appearance is noteworthy, especially his observation that she physically represents both order (her hair) and anger (her "dread" disposition). This tension persists in the realm of her domestic existence: she is alone (and presumably lonely), and despite her "excessive" capacity for love, she is unable to sustain a relationship and keep a companion. Like Calypso, Tia Dalma has a seductive allure that dominates her identity; it is a crucial element of the plot in the first three *Pirates of the Caribbean* films.

Her sexuality remains relevant when she is finally freed from her human body. The ritual involves someone saying the words "Calypso, I release you from your human bonds," but most importantly, these words "must be spoken as if to a lover." The initial effort to complete the ritual is unsuccessful because the required words are not spoken with the appropriate sensuality, but when a different crew member warmly whispers to Tia Dalma, she closes her eyes as if in deep pleasure and then erupts into convulsions, exploding into a monsoon of small crabs, the entire response an approximation of a sexual climax. Tia Dalma's portrayal as a hypersexualized seductress traffics in the representational politics of both her race and gender. Her portrayal builds on the intersection of racial and gender stereotypes of black women that suggest they are licentious and in a sustained condition of sexual availability. In the essay "Selling Hot Pussy: Representations of Black Female Sexuality in the Cultural Marketplace," bell hooks explores the eroticization of black women, particularly performers. For example, she discusses the African American entertainer Josephine Baker, whose erotic dance routines, performed mainly in Paris from the late 1920s through the 1940s, emphasized her buttocks, and maintains that this emphasis was a method of taking advantage of white assumptions regarding black female sexuality. Hooks asserts that black women's sexuality is a dominant constituent of their public profiles, and that "the black female body gains attention only when it is synonymous with accessibility, availability, when it is sexually deviant."[42] Stereotypical assumptions about Tia Dalma's race and gender help facilitate the construction of her persona as a hypersexualized, seductive heartbreaker who has done irreparable damage to Davy Jones.

It is Jones, the monstrous captain of the ghost ship *Flying Dutchman*, and not Sparrow, who was most subject to Tia Dalma's seduction. Many years earlier, while in his human form, Davy Jones fell hopelessly in love with the goddess Calypso. She assigned him the task of guiding the souls of the dead who were lost at sea, and promised that if he did this job, every ten years the two of them could be together for one day. When the appointed time arrived a decade later, Calypso did not fulfill her promise, and Jones was both devastated and enraged. In revenge, he convinced the Brethren Court of pirates to bind her in human form as Tia Dalma, which brought her control of the seas to an end. He also removed his heart, placed it in a chest, and hid the chest away so that he could no longer be hurt. He then transformed himself into a grotesque monster, his external persona mirroring the anger and heartbreak he felt inside. As Sparrow anticipated, Tia Dalma was able to explain the origins and purpose of the key that had led him to seek her out: it opens the chest that holds Jones's heart, enables a range of powerful opportunities for the person who possesses it, and can save Sparrow from one hundred years of servitude to Davy Jones. Jones, like Sparrow, sports locks, represented as a mass of tentacles on his head. These tentacle-locks situate Jones, like Sparrow, as a rude boy and an outlaw, an identity that follows him into the afterlife.

The similarly monstrous identity that Tia Dalma assumes is persistent in her portrayal throughout the series, her latent monstrosity reflected in traits such as her supernatural abilities, her unusual facial adornment, and her hair. In *The Monstrous-Feminine: Film, Feminism, Psychoanalysis*, Barbara Creed argues that "when woman is represented as monstrous it is almost always in relation to her mothering and reproductive functions."[43] She further asserts that classifications of the monstrous-feminine include "witches," the group that Tia Dalma would arguably fall into. As a witch, she occupies a permanently liminal position between the spirit and material worlds, between monstrous goddess and human. Her true identity as Calypso, a vengeful goddess who takes material form as a literal monster, towering several stories above the ship, obscures the audience's ability to read her black body as representing that of the slaves and other peoples of color tyrannized by the colonial experience in the Caribbean. Instead she is used to create a myth of white victimization and manipulation, brought about by her otherworldly seductive powers.

Furthermore, Davy Jones's relationship with Tia Dalma is a metonym for Europe's relationship with the region, and the *Pirates of the Caribbean* films invoke magic and mythology to help situate the region as enchanting and seductive, yet also foreboding and deadly. These characteristics conspire to render the Caribbean as feral, primitive, and menacing, deflecting the viewers' focus from Europe's barbaric colonial project in the region. Additionally, Tia Dalma–Calypso's potent and mythological seductiveness follows in a tradition of situating the Caribbean as enchanting and bewitching, rendering helpless those outsiders who dare come in contact with it. Like Sparrow and Davy Jones, these outsiders become powerless to resist their infatuation with the region. Descriptions of the Caribbean in these ethereal terms began with Christopher Columbus who, in his now-infamous letter to Luis de Santangel, describes it as surreal and mythical.[44]

Portrayals of the Caribbean as marvelous reality have been perpetuated from the time of western Europe's initial encounter with it, and this construction persists in the representation of Tia Dalma, reinvigorating historical efforts to pathologize the region and portray it (and other colonized spaces) as enchanted, seductive, and dangerous. In *Orientalism*, Edward Said suggests that classifying colonized groups as backward and irrational clears space for Western assumptions of superiority relative to those groups.[45] Furthermore, Kameelah Samuel argues that "Disney severs Tia Dalma from her African antecedents 'disneyfying' Vodun into a more palatable and safe form with which its audience is familiar."[46] But this familiarity that Disney counts on evolved within an established framework of strangeness. Thus, Tia Dalma's representation of the Caribbean and her immersion in magic and myth conspire to imply that the Caribbean is not only aberrant and freakish but also backward, suspending, in some respects, Western responsibility for the savage violence enacted against the region and its people.

Zombies

Like Vodun and Obeah, zombies have ancestral roots in the Caribbean and are probably the first Caribbean monster to make it into film; yet this monster is now primarily associated with the American cultural landscape. In *The Transatlantic Zombie*, Sarah Lauro notes the irony that the zombie is particularly well suited to be an American icon because of its immigrant status and its elided ancestry: "The zombie is perhaps the most 'American' monster: it comes from elsewhere, and it is distinctly informed by slavery, colonialism, and occupation, and yet somehow this always gets relegated to the backstory rather than treated as the story."[47] While the films I discuss are set in the region, and the ancestry of the zombie is apparent, the wave of zombie culture that has swept North America since the 1960s dislocates the zombie from its Caribbean roots. In the films produced since this period, the zombie is no longer a potent signifier of the Caribbean and is instead strongly representational of communal anxiety. Ann Kordas makes this point in the essay "New South, New Immigrants, New Women, New Zombies": "American popular culture, especially Hollywood films, transformed the Haitian zombie into a creature that revealed more about the hopes and fears lurking in the American psyche than in the Haitian one."[48]

Zombies are most often portrayed as beings trapped in a liminal space, somewhere between life and death. In early zombie movies, they are frequently associated with a misshapen representation of the Haitian practice of Vodun. There has been a proliferation of scholarship on cinematic zombies, much of it focused on iconic films such as George Romero's *Night of the Living Dead* (1968) and *Dawn of the Dead* (1978) as well as on more recent films such as *28 Days Later* (2002) and *Shaun of the Dead* (2004). Peter Dendle explains that Romero's zombie films and those that came after mark a distinct shift in the genre: "In earlier presentations, the zombie was a derivative creature, always under the control of some other more intelligent being (voodoo master, mad scientist, vampire). Romero liberated the zombie from the shackles of a master, and invested his zombies not with a function (a job or task such as zombies were standardly given by voodoo priests), but rather a drive (eating flesh)."[49] In addition to reshaping myths about zombie genesis, these very popular films, and indeed the majority of zombie films produced over the last fifty years, dislocate the zombie from its geographic and cultural Caribbean origins.

An increasing number of zombie scholars, such as Peter Dendle, Kyle Bishop, and Shawn McIntosh, do a thoughtful job of reclaiming the zombie's Caribbean heritage by explaining the etymology of the term and charting the evolution of zombie folklore in Haiti. This acknowledgment of the zombie's ancestry advances the scholarship in this genre and puts the zombie in its proper sociohistorical context, often leading to a recognition of how race is an underpinning theme in these narratives. For example, in "The Zombie as a Barometer of Cultural Anxiety," Peter Dendle notes that in some early films, zombies "serve essentially the same scapegoat function that African Americans do in Hollywood movies of the same period."[50] In "The Evolution of the Zombie," Shawn McIntosh acknowledges the racial tensions in some of the early zombie films from the 1930s and 1940s, which "touched on white/black racial issues." In addition, McIntosh points out that the Caribbean setting of these films provided a "wellspring of issues upon which to touch regarding the socioeconomic milieu of rich, white plantation owners and downtrodden black peasants and workers."[51]

I too am concerned with how zombie films engage with race and the Caribbean cultural landscape—specifically, how these films construct their monsters and which populations will be revealed when the monsters' costumes are ripped away. I focus mainly on the earliest zombie films, those produced during the nascent stages of the genre, in the 1930s and 1940s. These films, which are usually set in the Caribbean and engage with blackness and Afro-Caribbean culture, offer the most fertile cinematic field for exploring the zombie before its ties with the region were for the most part severed. I discuss *King of the Zombies* (1941), *White Zombie* (1932), and *I Walked with a Zombie* (1943). Set in the Caribbean, they were among the most popular of the first zombie films, and therefore provide a prime opportunity for the unmasking of some of Hollywood's earliest Caribbean monsters. All three films bear a striking resemblance to one another: they feature white women living in a sexually charged environment where they fall prey to a "voodoo" practitioner who then turns them into zombies. Additionally, the films pathologize the Caribbean, suggesting that it is deadly, contaminating, and unnatural.

Set on an unnamed Caribbean island, "probably somewhere between Cuba and Puerto Rico," *King of the Zombies* is the story of Bill Summers, a white governmental operative on a secret mission, and Jefferson Jackson, his black valet, who, along with their pilot, Mac, crash-land on this mysterious island after getting lost during a storm. They are taken in by Dr. Sangre, an Austrian refugee living on the island with his ailing wife, Alyce, and her niece, Barbara. Alyce is in a permanent trance: she never speaks or makes eye contact—just wanders the halls of their spooky mansion, dressed in opulent evening gowns. Sangre describes her condition as a "strange malady" that he claims he is "trying to cure." He further explains that "she lives, yet walks in the land of those beyond," implying that Alyce's condition is caused by the Caribbean, since her illness mysteriously came upon her when they arrived on the island.

It is eventually revealed that Sangre controls a cadre of zombie servants, and that he is spying for the Germans. He sends false radio signals, luring planes to crash, and then with the help of Tahama, an elderly black servant who is a voodoo priestess, he extracts intelligence from the minds of his crash victims and transfers that information into Alyce's head. When Alyce dies, at the end of the film, her mind and body completely exhausted from her husband's abuse, Sangre forces Barbara to become her aunt's replacement as a human hard drive, but she is saved by the American visitors.

White Zombie similarly features a white woman in distress. It begins as the story of Neil and Madeline, a young white couple in Haiti to get married. Their wealthy host, Charles Beaumont, who is in love with Madeline, asks a sinister figure named Murder Legendre to help him win her affection. Murder is the white owner of a local sugar mill that uses black and white zombie labor, and his proposed solution is to turn Madeline into a zombie. At first Charles rejects the plan, but eventually, out of a desperate yearning for Madeline's love, he complies with Murder's instructions and surreptitiously gives Madeline a potion that kills her. After her burial, he and Murder disinter her, and Murder turns her into a zombie who lives at his castle under his control. Meanwhile, Charles begins to regret his actions, commenting that he was "mad to do this." He further exclaims that Madeline's "soul is gone" and that he "can't bear those empty staring eyes." He ends up imploring Murder to return Madeline to her normal self, but Murder refuses.

Meanwhile, Madeline's husband, Neil, is devastated by her death and haunted by apparitions of her. When Neil becomes aware that her body has been removed from its tomb, he convinces Dr. Bruner, the missionary who married them, to accompany him to Murder's castle to investigate the unfolding mystery. In the end, Dr. Bruner (and Neil when he's not passed out) manages to rescue Madeline from her state of limbo.

Finally, *I Walked with a Zombie*, set on the fictional Caribbean island of St. Sebastian, is the story of Betsey, a Canadian nurse hired to care for Jessica, the ailing wife of Paul Holland, owner of a sugar plantation. Jessica wanders about the plantation great house in a catatonic state, yet she is always dressed to the nines, just like Madeline and Alyce. Jessica's physician explains that she has an incurable "tropical fever," and Betsy eventually comes to find out that Paul's half brother, Wesley, is in love with Jessica, and the sexual dynamics turn even more complicated when Betsey falls in love with Paul. Out of her love for Paul, Betsey becomes determined to help get Jessica better.

Mrs. Rand, Paul and Wesley's mother, is also the local pharmacist. Jessica goes to her to suggest that perhaps voodoo can cure Jessica, but Mrs. Rand strongly advises against it. Betsey ignores Mrs. Rand's advice and goes to a voodoo ceremony, only to make the shocking discovery that Mrs. Rand is the local voodoo priestess. It turns out that Jessica's condition was not caused by some unspecified "tropical fever" but by her mother-in-law, who had learned the voodoo arts and turned Jessica into a zombie when she found out Jessica was about to run off with her other son, Wesley. In the end, Wesley inadvertently kills Jessica and drowns himself.

The portrayal of zombies in all these films invites a postcolonial reading of the master-slave dialectic evoked by the zombie's relationship to its creator. The zombies, both black and white, are without agency and without voice. They lumber about, bodies erect and eyes empty, obeying the commands of the voodoo master who created them. Joan Dayan explains that "the phantasm of the zombie—a soulless husk deprived of freedom—is the ultimate sign of loss and dispossession."[52] While this observation certainly applies to early zombie films, my discussion centers on the portrayal of the white female zombies at the center of each narrative. These films depict white female sexuality as fragile—easily subject to corruption in the wrong (that is, black) environment. While the zombie white women may not hold key roles in these films, the plot of each hinges on efforts to reverse the desecration of their bodies and souls by the corrosive nature of the region. These white anxieties about black male access to white female bodies are aptly captured by Neil's comment "Better dead than that!" when he realizes that Madeline's missing body might be in the hands of the locals.

The femininity of the women is heightened, and so concomitantly is the horror of their white bodies being corrupted, by their being portrayed as the epitome of Western femininity. They roam about grand mansions, their slender bodies in the most sumptuous clothing, their hair impeccably coiffed and makeup meticulously applied. Even in slumber they are superbly dressed. For example, in *King of the Zombies*, when Alyce mindlessly wanders into Jeff's room, she is wearing an exotic sleeping ensemble that resembles wedding regalia. The outfit features billowy fabrics and a sleeping bonnet adorned with a train. Alyce's clothing sexualizes her and signals her heteronormativity. The women's reliance on someone to take care of them and a master to guide their actions marks their fragility as well as their compliance. Furthermore, they are silent throughout their tenure as zombies, unable to utter any expressions of agency.

These women's bodies are sexually charged, and the defenseless posture they assume as zombies facilitates all manner of sexually implied access to their bodies. For example, in *King of the Zombies*, Alyce's and Barbara's bodies are used as vessels for storing top-secret information intended to aid foreign enemies of the United States. In *White Zombie*, Charles helps turn Madeline into a zombie so that he can have the sexual access to her that he did not have while she was alive. When Murder refuses Charles's request to change her back, Madeline stands, staring blankly into space, while Murder lasciviously rubs her hands, practically drooling over her, his sexual intentions resonant throughout the scene. In *I Walked with a Zombie*, Jessica's body carries a heavy sexual charge that is rooted in the two brothers' competing love for her, and she was zombified to preserve her husband's exclusive sexual access to her.

Although the landscape and the black population of the region serve primarily as the backdrop against which these white dramas unfolds, the films nevertheless pathologize blackness and treat the Caribbean and its residents as corrupting forces that can create monsters of those within their reach. The films suggest that illness and disease abound in the islands, and the white people who come to the region may become contaminated because of their fragility; some are drawn to the region because they too are defective and latently monstrous. For example, in *King of the Zombies*, when Bill and his crew first arrive, Dr. Sangre tells them, "The slightest injury on this island often proves fatal," adding, "the climate" and "the evil spirits lurk here waiting to prey on the injured." Samantha, Sangre's servant, who is originally from Alabama and hence able to critique the island from the perspective of a black but non-Caribbean subject, also perpetuates this myth of the Caribbean as predator. She offers Jefferson a "magic potion" that, she claims, is for "scaring away the evil spirits." She suggestively adds, "The place is crawling with them, and that ain't all." Samantha explains that there are zombies around and then suggests that the Caribbean is an ideal environment for the festering of evil and unnaturalness: "This is where they [zombies] grows best."

Murder Legendre is as deadly as the Caribbean space constructed by these early zombie films and the source of most of the villainy in *White Zombie*. While the film does not include explicit commentary about the deadliness of the landscape, that deadliness is embodied by Murder. He is closely tied to Haiti because he lives there and runs a local sugar mill. Additionally, he has mastered voodoo and controls a plethora of zombies that inhabit the landscape. These zombies include several public figures who were once his enemies, such as the minister of the interior and the executioner. Murder's ties to Haiti as well as his control over former members of Haiti's government firmly connect his identity with that of the region. In *I Walked with a Zombie*, the Caribbean space is again implicated as deadly. While escorting Betsey to St. Sebastian, Paul notices her marveling at the ocean and immediately dispels any notions of the Caribbean being tranquil and inviting. "There is no beauty here—only death and decay," he warns before going on to explain, "Everything good dies here—even the stars." Additionally, Jessica's doctor alleges that her illness was caused by the region when he explains that she contracted an incurable "tropical fever."

While the obvious monsters are present in these films in the form of zombies both black and white, the looming monster is the region itself. Furthermore, when the monster is unmasked, the identity hidden underneath the elaborate costuming of sickness and decay is black and male. The male identity of the region is asserted through the villainous or corrupting male forces that are firmly connected with the region. (While Jessica's husband

and brother-in-law are not portrayed as villainous, they are the source of her corruption.) Sangre, Murder, Charles, Paul, and Wesley have strong Caribbean identities because they live in the region and earn a living from the land. Murder, Charles, and the Holland family own sugar mills and plantations—holdovers from the days of slavery—and Sangre lures planes to crash and effectively merge with the land. Although Sangre is not a native of the region, it has become his home by default because he is a refugee without a passport.

These men are also coded as black because of the ways that race underpins the portrayal of the region via its association with slave labor and Afro-Caribbean spiritual practices. In fact, in *I Walked with a Zombie*, it is revealed that the Holland family brought slaves to the island, and a statue in the courtyard of the Holland great house is the masthead from a slave ship. The zombie in these early films deflects attention from the way the region itself is rendered as a monstrosity and averts the audience's gaze from the trauma caused by the Caribbean's colonial encounter, which is seen in the poverty and abysmal working conditions of the poor black islanders.

Peter Dendle suggests that "the zombie can be read as tracking a wide range of cultural, political, and economic anxieties of American society."[53] These films were made when Jim Crow practices flourished in the United States and in a milieu laden with white anxieties about racial intermixing. These white anxieties about miscegenation were apparent in Hollywood from at least the time of *Birth of a Nation* (1915), which, in its revisionist history of the United States, constructs the black man as morally and sexually corrupt.

Elizabeth Young makes a similar argument about the way race is coded in film when she suggests that the monster in *Bride of Frankenstein* is coded as black. For example, she asserts that the "mutilated and dismembered parts of corpses" which constitute the body of the monster emblematize "the frequent mutilation and dismembering of lynching victims."[54] Chera Kee explains that anxieties about race were mediated by the presence of Vodun in early zombie films, and she suggests that the films were unlikely to "cast a black man as the corrupting force and the white woman as susceptible to his advances"; instead, black zombies were used as "background and filler, and it was the 'black' magic of Haitian Voodoo, utilized by zombie masters, that openly threatened white femininity."[55]

It is significant that in Western popular culture, the monster most closely associated with the Caribbean in ancestry (though not necessarily in contemporary cultural awareness) emerged from Haiti, the country that launched the only successful slave revolt that resulted in the creation of a black republic in the New World. The European imperialist powers were unsettled by Haiti's symbolic value, as Wade Davis explains in *Passage of Darkness*: "In the nineteenth century Haiti's very existence was a constant thorn in the side of an imperialistic age."[56] Kee makes the connection between the early portrayal of zombies in American popular culture and America's political relationship to Haiti: "Early zombie fiction in the United States owes much to fears of Haiti as an independent black republic.... Anxiety about Haiti in the United States translated into an anxiety about Voodoo."[57] My argument is that this anxiety informs the construction of both zombies and the Caribbean in the films discussed above, and is reflected in the coding of the region as monstrous.

Gangster Monsters

Supernatural crime thrillers that implicate Afro-Caribbean spirituality in the making of outlaws and gangsters make up another category of films that feature Caribbean monsters. This discussion focuses on *Live and Let Die* (1973), *Predator* (1987), *Predator II* (1990), *Marked for Death* (1990), and *Bad Boys II* (2003), all movies featuring a Caribbean villain immersed in magic. Gruesome murderers and devilish villains who derive their power from perverted imaginings of Afro-Caribbean spiritual practices are common elements in all these films, along with copious amounts of blood, gore, and chanting devotees. The "gangster monsters" in each film are sites of excess—corporeal and behavioral—and though they may not necessarily have a distinct monstrous physiology, their monstrosity manifests as a merger of their aberrant behavior with malevolent supernatural alliances. The result is characters that are magically invincible and intriguing as well as extraordinarily brutal. Gangster monsters are black Caribbean criminals who traffic in drugs and sorcery, two illicit activities locked in a disturbing embrace. The monsters repel and attract simultaneously, and they are framed within the classic gaze of horror audiences, one that is disturbed by grotesque creatures but compelled to observe their grotesque behavior. For my purposes, perhaps the most noteworthy similarity among these villains is that they are a black alien presence—specifically, a Caribbean one—in the United States, and so the films engage in a long-running conversation about immigration and race while diverting attention from the oppressive socioeconomic circumstances that nurture criminal behavior in general and specifically in the Caribbean.

Live and Let Die is the eighth movie in the James Bond series. It stars Roger Moore as the omnicompetent spy created by Ian Fleming in his novels. Set in New York, New Orleans, and the fictional Caribbean island of San Monique, *Live and Let Die* is the story of James Bond's mission to investigate the deaths of a British agent in each of these locations. Agent 007's inquiry leads him to a villainous Caribbean dictator, Dr. Kananga (played by Yaphet Kotto), and a ruthless drug baron, Mr. Big, whom we later find out are the same person. Kananga conducts a lucrative multinational enterprise with branches in the three primary settings of the film, all of them important cultural centers of the African diaspora in the New World. Additionally, he is immersed in the occult and characterized as associated with Vodun. As 007 shuttles among these sites, he charms women out of their bell-bottoms and defeats death as he exposes Kananga's corruption.

Marked for Death also features a cadre of immigrant bad guys who use magic in their illegal drug activities. The story begins with a recently retired DEA operative named John Hatcher (played by Steven Seagal) returning to his hometown in the suburban neighborhood of Lincoln Heights, near Chicago. Hatcher realizes that his formerly wholesome hometown is plagued by a scourge of drugs and violence inflicted by a Jamaican drug posse. He ends up intervening when the posse and other area drug dealers get into a vicious shootout at a bar. In retaliation, the posse carries out a drive-by shooting at his home. His niece is wounded, and scrawled on the floor of his home is what a police expert describes as a "black magic" ideogram indicating he has been "marked for death." Incensed and inflated with righteous anger, Hatcher begins an all-out battle with the posse and its leader, Screwface, a mystical practitioner of the dark arts who uses his magical skills to aid his illegal activities. With the assistance of his pal Max, an African American football coach at the local high school, Hatcher initiates what becomes a transnational pursuit of Screwface that takes him and Max all the way to Jamaica. Hatcher manages to kill Screwface, only to return to the United States and find out that the dead man has a twin and that he has to effectively kill Screwface a second time.

Predator II similarly features a Jamaican drug cartel. The film is set in Los Angeles, which is under siege as a brutal turf war takes place between Jamaican and Colombian drug gangs. The Jamaican cartel, known as King Willie's Voodoo Posse, assaults and murders the leader of the Colombian cartel in a ritual that involves hanging the Colombian gang leader upside down, painting his naked body with blood, and removing his heart. But before members of the posse can leave the scene of the crime, they become the prey of an unidentifiable monster that skins them and hangs them upside down. A police officer named Michael Harrigan (played by Danny Glover) investigates these murders. Harrigan enlists the help of King Willie, a dreadlocked magical figure and leader of the Jamaican posse. King Willie tells Harrigan that the monster is "supernatural" shortly before falling victim to it. As the film concludes, Harrigan realizes that the murders are the work of a cyborg, an alien being who is part flesh and part machine. Harrigan eventually kills it.

That the gangster monsters in all three films are black is apparent: Kananga's, Screwface's, and King Willie's race is immediately recognizable, and their status as alien Caribbean nationals is established early. In *Marked for Death* and *Predator II*, the polluting and infesting quality of this presence is emphasized. In *Predator II*, a newscaster reports that "bloodthirsty Jamaican and Colombian drug lords have spoilt a once fine city." In *Marked for Death*, one of the early scenes features white high school students being offered drugs by black Jamaican posse members who have infiltrated their presumably pristine white space. A police officer describes the posse as "spreading out," noting its unwanted intrusion. In *Live and Let Die*, this kind of infiltration is implied in how blackness is pathologized. The characters of the two gangster monsters are merged: Kananga, a Caribbean head of state, and Mr. Big, an African American drug baron, are the same person, suggesting that the deviant and degenerative behavior associated with black men is uninterrupted by geographic and national divides.

I include the cyborg in *Predator II* among these gangster monsters. While his parallel status as an alien intruder is evident, his blackness is less visible but nevertheless implied. For most of the film, he maintains a camouflage of invisibility; he manifests mostly as muffled utterances and a faint outline. But he is eventually revealed to be an extremely tall humanlike being with reptilian skin and the face of an insect, his blackness and Caribbean-ness most directly implied by a mass of tentacles on his head that approximate dreadlocks. These tentacles behave like locks, shifting and swaying as he moves, and more importantly, they are adorned with beads in much the way that King Willie's locks are adorned with a variety of ornaments. In fact, the Predator is like King Willie and his gang in other respects and functions as a bit of a doppelganger: like the posse members, the Predator hangs his victims upside down and uses Western sayings. At the start of the movie, one of King Willie's posse members says, "Shit happens," just before murdering his victim, and near the end of the movie, when the Predator is precariously hanging from the ledge of a building, he says, "Shit happens." The Predator carries weapons that although technologically advanced, resemble a spear and a disc. These weapons serve to tribalize and, consequently, racialize him. Additionally, for this installment in the series, the Predator was redesigned with "more tribal ornamentation on the forehead."[58]

Predator, the first film in the series, also codes the alien as Caribbean because the tentacles on his head again resemble dreadlocks. But this film seems more invested in pathologizing blackness generally. It not only racializes the deadly alien, which wreaks havoc in a South American jungle, but also constructs the two black male characters in problematic ways. *Predator* stars Arnold Schwarzenegger as Dutch, who, along with his special operations team, ends up in a fierce battle with the extraterrestrial creature, which preys on humans for sport. Dillon (played by Carl Weathers) and Mac (played by Bill Duke) are two black men on Dutch's team, and in a nod to the figure of the self-denying "darkie" servant of past film eras, they both sacrifice themselves for the good of the team. Furthermore, Adilifu Nama argues that the men are "reductively frame[d] . . . as phallic objects that require containment" and notes that because only the black men can "'see' the 'invisible' alien," they have an affinity with it.[59]

Toward the end of the film, Dutch is the only member of the team left, and to better stalk the alien, he coats himself in mud as camouflage and becomes part of the feral jungle landscape. This assumption of temporary metaphorical blackness is key to his eventual triumph over the Predator and further confirms that the alien is coded as black, since the assumption of a similar racial identity is necessary in order to effectively combat him. The alien and aberrant status of the Predator and the inability to define him by using conventional identifiers of race and ethnicity are emphasized by a repeated rhetorical question in the film: "Who the hell are you?"

Bad Boys II likewise situates the black male body as alien. Set in Miami, the film stars Martin Lawrence and Will Smith as police officers Marcus Barnett and Mike Lowrey, who are hot on the trail of Haitian and Cuban drug dealers. The title of the film readily exposes its intent to indict the black Caribbean male, because of the title's association with the reggae hit "Bad Boys" by Inner Circle. Made famous as the song that opens the TV series *Cops*, "Bad Boys" is a warning to Caribbean gangsters to beware the consequences of their illicit activities: "Bad boys, bad boys / Whatcha gonna do, whatcha gonna do / When they come for you?" Similarly, the film suggests that certain doom is in store for Caribbean aliens who trespass on U.S. soil and engage in illegal activities. As in *Predator II* and *Marked for Death*, the Caribbean gangsters are pathologized and constructed as a plague. This perspective is clearly articulated by the police chief, who says, "I do not want these animals taking over my city." While Cuba and the Cuban gang leader are portrayed as corrupt and demented, the supernatural is mobilized in the portrayal of the Haitian gang.

Icepick, the black informer who provides police with the location of the Haitian gang, is himself suffused in magic. Icepick's yard features a variety of crosses buried in the ground, in an eerie approximation of a graveyard. But the crosses are adorned with items such as dolls hanging upside down, chairs, bottles, and candles; additionally, a flock of chickens is roaming among the crosses, which further animates the entire scene with strong undertones of Afro-Caribbean spiritual practices such as Santeria, in which chickens are used in sacrificial rites. Inside his house, Icepick operates a botanica that is brimming with items such as religious statues, money candles, and incense. After coercing Icepick to reveal the location of the Haitian gang, Barnett and Lowrey launch an assault on the premises where gang members are in hiding: a building with a sign that indicates it was once a Haitian cultural center.

That the headquarters of the gang is in a location identified with an entire culture indicates the center's metonymic function as a nationally representative site. Inside the headquarters, the mise-en-scène delivers a sinister portrait of Vodun. The camera pans around the poorly lit space to reveal numerous altars adorned with glowing candles, skulls, and statues of saints; some altars are crosses festooned like those in Icepick's yard. By suffusing the space with iconography that alludes to Vodun and other Afro-Caribbean spiritual practices, the film, like *Predator II* and *Marked for Death*, intimates that the criminal activity of these Caribbean gangster monsters is intricately associated with cultural practices of the region. When the assault ensues and the Haitians begin firing from one section of the house, the blond-dreadlocked gang leader shouts, "Who is in my house?" In the conversation that follows, Lowrey reinforces the alien status of the Haitians and rebuts their claim to U.S. territory by retorting, "You in my country!"

Additionally, *Bad Boys II* symbolically gestures toward zombification with its proliferation of partially dead bodies: live bodies brought to the brink of death through tainted batches of the drug Ecstasy as it circulates in the streets of Miami. Furthermore, dead bodies are given new lives as vessels for the illegal transportation of drugs.

The same construction of the black Caribbean male pervades *Live and Let Die*, *Predator II*, *Marked for Death*, and *Bad Boys II*. The gangster monsters constitute an alien Caribbean presence that is further established by associating them with potent, albeit inaccurately rendered, cultural symbols of the region. The most prolific of these symbols, and the source of my interest in the films, is the magico-religious practices with which they are affiliated. These practices are suggested and described in a variety of ways. For example, Kananga and his drug enterprise are steeped in magic, and he exploits the superstitions of the San Monique natives by using Vodun-inflected lore to divert attention from his heroin-smuggling activities. Mechanized graves make ghouls magically appear, and replicas of shrunken heads camouflage cameras and guns. These contraptions invoke magic by creating the illusion that supernatural forces are in cahoots with Kananga, but the real magic is the concealment of his illegal activities. He also operates the Oh Cult Voodoo Store, and one of his henchmen is named Baron Samedi (the Vodun loa associated with the world of spirits and graveyards), a quasi-magical figure. In an extension of this construction of his supernatural ability, Kananga holds a young white woman named Solitaire captive in order to exploit her psychic abilities. Known to possess the "power of the Obeah," Solitaire is a psychic and tarot card reader played by Jane Seymour. She is kept under close watch by Kananga, who believes that her magical abilities will be compromised if she loses her virginity. It is within this complex milieu of race, sexuality, and the fantastic that Agent 007's mission unfolds.

The 1933 film *The Emperor Jones* starring Paul Robeson is the cinematic predecessor of *Live and Let Die* and also suggests the impotency of black political leadership. *The Emperor Jones*, based loosely on the play of the same name by Eugene O'Neill, portrays a despotic black leader of a Caribbean island who uses the illusion of magic to exercise power over his subjects. The film's protagonist is a black Pullman porter named Brutus Jones, played by Robeson. Jones is from a small town, but his job on the railroad exposes him to cosmopolitan enclaves in the city, where he succumbs to the lure of gambling and sex. After stabbing someone in a fight, he ends up on a chain gang, but escapes and finds work on a ship. While passing a Caribbean island, Jones jumps overboard and swims to shore. He tricks the unsophisticated leader of the island out of his throne by making the false claim that he has magical abilities and can be killed only by a silver bullet. As emperor, he increases taxes and brings sophistication to the kingdom: he has the palace luxuriously decorated, and he and his court begin dressing in garish garments meant to approximate the clothing worn by royalty. But his reign is short. His subjects abandon him and launch an insurgency, and he descends into madness, haunted by ghosts from his past. He ends up being shot and killed by the rebels.

Like *Live and Let Die*, *The Emperor Jones* asserts the impotency of black male leadership and suggests that even when given access to the material wealth and power yearned after by marginalized populations, black men are unable to manage those resources. Jones fails as a Pullman porter, a coveted job for black men at the time, and also fails as a political leader. Furthermore, the film again associates the Caribbean with the supernatural and uses this association to comment on blacks in two ways. First, magic in the film suggests that black people are naïve and gullible, falling for Jones's pretend magic, and the film implies that the Caribbean is a malevolent and vengeful space where magic will manifest to exact retribution on wrongdoers. *The Emperor Jones* positions Africa as the source of the magic that pervades the Caribbean. It opens and closes with tribal scenes, people dancing and chanting, drums beating. At the start of the film, the tribal scene collapses into one at an animated service in a black church in Jones's hometown, suggesting that the black church is associated African tribal practices (a claim with some merit). Additionally, at the end of the film, images of this tribal scene and the haunting are interspersed, again mystifying Africa.

Just as Brutus Jones is associated with African-derived spiritual practices, Screwface and King Willie are connected with Vodun. A police analyst claims that an ideogram left at a crime scene by Screwface's gang is a "black magic" symbol, and a reporter refers to it as a "voodoo sign that signals the presence of the posse." King Willie is referred to as the "voodoo priest of the L.A. posse," and a police officer describes the posse's ritualistic murder of the Colombian drug lord as a "voodoo ritual" that she has seen before. At one point, Screwface's gang captures Hatcher's sister, and Screwface begins to perform a ritual by painting blood on her body, but he is interrupted and she escapes. Furthermore, most of the gang leaders have some kind of capacity to foretell the future. Kananga relies on the white psychic he holds captive; Screwface and King Willie are versed in the Yoruban divination practice of Ifá, the casting and interpreting of collections of objects to reveal information—in the films, they both use bones.

All of the films invoke Vodun as the spiritual practice that empowers and protects the gangster monsters. These filmic representations of Vodun often conflate it with Obeah and other Afro-Caribbean religions, a practice of amalgamation that started during slavery and still continues. Furthermore, the representations of Vodun in film often reflect a misunderstanding of the religion. Margarite Olmos and Lizabeth Paravasini-Gebert argue that "the practice of magic and sorcery is peripheral to Haitian Vodun," and explain that many of the anxieties about "Vodun beliefs and religious practices are conjured up by detractors of Vodun to prove the primitiveness and ignorance of this religious practice."[60] The result is that the affiliation of the gangster monsters with Vodun and other Afro-Caribbean religions pathologizes them and insists that they are markedly different from American religious practices.

The Caribbean identity of the gangster monsters is further asserted by the dreadlocks worn by Screwface, King Willie, most of their gang members, the Haitian gang leader in *Bad Boys II*, and most of his cronies, visually emphasizing their association with the region through their embodied disposition. Caribbean identity itself is rendered suspect because the gangster monsters are allied with Caribbean black power movements such as Rastafarianism that celebrate African identity, although the vicious and corrupt criminal activities of the gangster monsters clash with the basic tenets of Rastafarianism.[61] M. Kuumba and Femi Ajanaku contend that "dreadlocks became symbolic accompaniment to oppositional collective identities associated with the African liberation/Black Power movements."[62]

Screwface is depicted as allied with Rastafarianism through the images and quotations inscribed on the walls of his headquarters. The image of a Bob Marley–esque figure is surrounded by a number of fists raised in a black power salute. Slogans on the wall proclaim, "Victory Free African Dis R Time," "Bungi Man Fawad Fi Riva," and "Struggle Continue." Use of these phrases, misspellings and all, is an effort to mark Screwface's den as a black liberationist space and to undermine the viability of this ideology by constructing it as intimately yoked to criminal activity and suggesting that supporters of this political stance are illiterate. While Kananga is not dreadlocked, he represents the important moment in African diasporic history when black heads of state emerged after countries in the Caribbean and Africa gained their independence. These leaders included Eric Williams, prime minister of Trinidad and Tobago; Michael Manley, prime minister of Jamaica; Kwame Nkrumah, prime minister of Ghana; and Léopold Sédar Senghor, president of Senegal. Depicting Kananga as a drug baron at this important juncture in black world politics suggests that independence movements across the diaspora produced corrupt and incompetent leaders; and this association is similar to the suggestion that Rastafarianism spawned drug lords who seamlessly integrated their criminal activities with their religious faith.

In *Predator II*, *Marked for Death* and *Bad Boys II*, the presence of male African American protagonists complicates in intriguing ways the construction of Caribbean banditry associated with the villains, and negates any impulse to collapse all the black male characters into a single representational role. This nuanced portrayal of blackness in many ways underscores the films' treatment of the Caribbean as a contaminating agent, its monstrous impact highlighted by the casting of "uncontaminated" black males as adversaries of the gangster monsters. These counterpart roles imply the normalizing or perhaps purifying attributes of Americanness, even on black male bodies. These bodies not only deny a proclivity toward monstrous embodiment, unlike their Caribbean counterparts, but also function as agents combatting monstrosity, perhaps to keep at bay their own looming transmutation into monsters as black men in the New World.

In 1857, the U.S. Supreme Court's decision in *Dred Scott v. Sandford* spelled out that African Americans had no rights to citizenship, and though this ruling was nullified by the Thirteenth, Fourteenth, and Fifteenth Amendments, Jim Crow laws passed in the aftermath of Reconstruction, buoyed by individual and institutional racism, put those rights in jeopardy. Throughout American history, black identity has often collided with American identity. That collision was evident in the suspicions raised about the authenticity of President Barack Obama's birth certificate. Perhaps the African American characters in the films discussed here, aware of this troubled racial history, engage in the expulsion of Caribbean villains as a projected act of expelling their own undesirable racialized identity. In "Performing Whiteness: Naturalization Litigation and the Construction of Racial Identity in America," John Tehranian argues that the rejection of nonwhite identities is required of immigrants seeking American citizenship, helping underscore the unacceptability to the American body politic of black immigrant bodies: "The potential for immigrants to assimilate within mainstream Anglo-American culture was put on trial. Successful litigants demonstrated evidence of whiteness in their character, religious practices and beliefs, class orientation, language, ability to intermarry, and a host of other traits that had nothing to do with intrinsic racial grouping. Thus, a dramaturgy of whiteness emerged, responsive to the interests of society as defined by the class in power."[63] The competing roles of African American characters in the films under discussion are thus complicated by the ways that both race and immigration status intersect on the site of the immigrant bodies of black men.

A study of the representation of immigrants in the media conducted by the Opportunity Agenda, a social-justice communication lab based in New York, suggests that the American media helps reify assumptions that immigrant bodies are deviant. This study focused on "the representation and dominant storylines associated with immigration, immigrants, and immigrant and border communities within popular television programs during the April 2014 to June 2016 television seasons."[64] The study concluded: "Storylines about unlawful activities accounted for 25 percent of storylines involving immigrant characters. These storylines depicted immigrant characters directly participating in unlawful activities or being questioned by police, often as a direct result of their status as an immigrant." This study demonstrates that the tendency to link immigrants with lawlessness is not only common in current political debates about immigration but also evident in the popular media. This portrayal of immigrants as deviant, however, is upended by research showing that immigrants are less likely than U.S. citizens to be involved in criminal behavior. A 2017 study by the Cato Institute, a conservative think tank, makes this point: "By race and ethnicity, every group of legal and illegal immigrants has a lower incarceration rate than their native peers. Even the incarceration rate for illegal immigrants is lower than the incarceration rate for native white Americans."[65]

Criminal behavior of the kind seen in the films is legendary in the Caribbean, specifically Jamaica. Numerous books, including Laurie Gunst's *Born Fi' Dead*, Ian Thomson's *The Dead Yard*, and Deborah Thomas's *Exceptional Violence*, explore the criminal underworld in the island and unmask the subterranean factors contributing to the emergence of the transnational narcotics trade and its control by drug cartels, or posses. Gunst offers a much more nuanced perspective than the films on these criminal activities, implicating the United States and international organizations such as the World Bank and the International Monetary Fund in the onslaught of violence that hit the island in the early 1970s. She lists a number of events—the IMF's devaluation of the island's currency; a sharp decline in tourism, facilitated by a tarnished image courtesy of the American press; the corruption of elected leaders; and the illegal sale of guns from the United States—that a contributed to the sharp upswing in violence.[66] This is the violence of which Peter Tosh spoke in his speech at the One Love Peace Concert. Gunst adds that international policies affecting Jamaica were driven by concerns having little to do with the island itself: "Jamaica became yet another theater of the worldwide cold war. The island's contortions were a claustrophobic replay of those in Chile, in Nicaragua, in a dozen other outposts of strife where the superpowers played out their East-West death dance." Gangsters emerged in Jamaica in the 1970s as bastard arms of political parties. They were seen as expendable: politicians discarded them, and police "gunned them down when their brief period of usefulness was over." Some eventually made their way to the streets of America.

In *Exceptional Violence*, Thomas offers a similarly insightful exploration of violence in Jamaica, and like Gunst, she demystifies the roots of the islands disturbingly high murder rate. When her book was published (2011), the Caribbean had "a murder rate higher than any other region in the world," and Jamaica competed with South Africa and Colombia as the country with the highest.[67] In addition to the politically sanctioned gang violence that erupted in the 1970s, Thomas implicates Jamaica's massive debt, which was the "fourth highest per capita in the world," and the island's high unemployment rate for young men and women—32.9 percent and 43.7 percent. Thomas specifically addresses the claim the films all seem to make about the aberrance of Caribbean citizens, an aberrance transmogrified by the infusion of magic. She explains that among some scholars—and in my opinion, among the public at large within and beyond the Caribbean—the ongoing assumption has been that "the perpetrators of . . . violence are seen as immutably bereft of moral responsibility or human empathy, and their behavior is seen to be patterned by a pathological culture that they cannot help but reproduce." To dispel these assumptions, her study argues that "violence is generally *not* a cultural phenomenon but an effect of class formation, a process that is immanently racialized and gendered." The portrayal of Caribbean gangster monsters in the films discussed here demonstrates the precise absence of nuance to which Thomas refers—these films are undergirded by the assumption that the criminal behavior portrayed is native to the black and Caribbean bodies of the perpetrators; that presumed pathology is what manifests in the monstrous embodiment of the criminals.

The gangster monsters, Tia Dalma, and the earliest cinematic zombies offer examples of how Hollywood uses monstrosity to camouflage identity. As Bellin suggests, monstrosity enhances our suspicions about outsiders, particularly when they are ethnic minorities, while distracting us from the immediate issues that circumscribe the dialogue on immigration, such as poverty, political oppression, and the legacy of slavery and colonialism. The films discussed here participate in the creation of Caribbean monsters, and the unmasking of these thinly veiled monsters seems to reveal levels of anxiety about Caribbean bodies and indeed the region.

CHAPTER THREE

The Haunting of a Nation

Death and Discourse in Jamaica

> Ghosts are there in the blood of the living, ghosts
> of the living past and unborn future.
>
> WILSON HARRIS

This chapter is concerned with death, particularly reports of encounters between the embodied and the disembodied. It focuses on three allegedly factual reports of Jamaican hauntings that have acquired national renown. What does it mean when stories of hauntings become nationally told narratives that rise to the forefront of a nation's consciousness? With countless stories of hauntings in circulation, what causes just a handful to resonate within a nation, energizing the dead with new life? This chapter considers how these narratives comment on the region's legacy of imperialism and internal deterioration, specifically on how Caribbean cosmologies as well as the particularities of the socioeconomic and political moment that produced these hauntings inform their character.

The ghost story genre is an ancient form of cultural expression. From the Old Testament story about the Witch of Endor summoning the ghost of Samuel to modern hauntings featured on U.S. television series such as *The Haunting of . . .* (2012–16), stories that exploit the tension between life and death, being and nonbeing, embodiment and disembodiment, are everywhere. The Caribbean is replete with ghosts, and stories about them. In the introduction to the anthology *The Haunted Tropics: Caribbean Ghost Stories*, the editor, Martin Munro states: "Every island of the Caribbean is the site of a deep haunting. . . . Given the history of the Caribbean, it is not surprising that much of the region's literature bears a haunted quality: ghosts are everywhere, be they of the Amerindians, the African ancestors, the slaves, the planters, the indentured workers, the victims of dictatorships, foreign invasions and natural disasters, or the modern exiles."[1] Ghost stories (in the Caribbean context, replace "ghost" with "duppy," "jumbie," or "*fantom*") occupy a shadowy narrative space, often straddling the categories of folklore, myth, and legend. I use the term "ghost story" to refer to any account of a supernatural incident situated by the narrative as true.

A few distinctions need to be made. Some stories about what we would consider a paranormal event take the form of a folktale. An example is the story of the Jamaican heroine Nanny of the Maroons, said to have been able to catch bullets with her buttocks. Another is the story of the Bermudian slave Sally Bassett, burnt at the stake in the eighteenth century for her alleged involvement in an effort to poison her owners. Bermuda's national flower is said to have grown from her ashes.[2] Stories about the paranormal that circulate as folktales are generally understood as fictional and do not inspire debate. Few people would argue that Nanny could actually catch a bullet with her buttocks or that the Bermudian national flower spontaneously generated itself in the aftermath of Sally Bassett's murder.

On the other hand, some stories about the paranormal circulate as truth, and these are the ones in which I am interested. For example, in St. Lucia, stories of small creatures called boloms are well known. They are said to hatch from an egg tucked under the arm of the person who becomes the master of the bolom, which lives only on raw meat and does the bidding of its master as long as it is kept fed.[3] A 2013 newspaper article in *Dominica News Online* relates the unexplainable presence of someone thought to be a bolom in a St. Lucian man's selfie taken when no one else was around.[4] To interpret stories of hauntings like that one, theorists mobilize specific critical approaches.

Theoretical Approaches to Hauntings

For example, the internationally renowned folklorist Linda Dégh regards ghost stories like the ones discussed in this chapter as a type of legend, and she defines a legend as a "narrative response" to some form of "stimulus."[5]

Dégh argues that a key characteristic of ghost stories, and legends in general, is that they are a contested narrative: "The legend is a legend once it entertains debate about belief . . . about one's own or someone else's experience." This characteristic is defining: "The sounding of contrary opinion is what makes a legend a legend." This state of contestation is important because it is an indicator of a ghost story's unstable nature as neither fully truth nor fiction, and this element of its definition distinctly separates it from folklore.[6] The way in which ghost stories hover in a liminal space between fact and fiction is perhaps the characteristic that has made these stories so compelling over the ages—they force us to question our beliefs about our understanding of the world and what we consider possible.

Dégh, along with several other scholars, see ghost stories as a potent window into the culture from which they emerge. Her focus on these stories came about because of this realization, which was made against the backdrop of modernity and the social changes it has produced. According to Dégh, legends are "the most reliable barometer of human concerns in an age when fundamental changes in social relationships have been speedily, aggressively imposed by electrification of communication technology."[7] Jeannie Thomas perceives ghost stories similarly, suggesting that they "help us look more closely and analytically at culture, the environment, and the personal"; specifically, "Ghost stories reveal how culture manifests itself in a twilight world that makes copious room for uncertainty and possibility."[8] For example, in *Ghosts and the Japanese: Cultural Experience in Japan's Death Legends*, Michiko Iwasaka and Barre Toelken explain that Japanese ghost stories reflect that culture's belief in traditional formalities: "In literary terms, it is nearly irrelevant whether people actually believe a spirit can return, or if the ghosts are 'simply' the public dramatization of guilt felt by survivors: the ghost legends are powerful expressions of the obligations and niceties which the Japanese feel are incumbent upon themselves as they lead normal, acceptable lives within their culture."[9] Some scholars advocate an even more explicit perspective on the value of ghost stories.

In the essay "The Popularity of Paranormal Experiences in the United States," William MacDonald suggests that belief in "paranormal" events is a result of our efforts to deal with human "crises." Among other things, these events help us feel a sense of "control" over our lives and all their unpredictable and unmanageable occurrences.[10] Following a similar line of argument,

Gillian Bennett asserts that belief in the supernatural can be a strategy for giving order to chaos,[11] and Barbara Walker argues that the concept of the supernatural facilitates our ability to include "inexplicable things" in the arena of our human experience.[12] All these scholars recognize the latent value of stories about the supernatural.

Cathy Caruth's ideas about the impact of trauma offer another lens through which to contemplate stories of hauntings. Caruth explains that in relation to post-traumatic stress disorder, "most descriptions generally agree that there is a response, sometimes delayed, to an overwhelming event or events, which takes the form of repeated, intrusive hallucinations, dreams, thoughts or behaviors stemming from the event."[13] These manifestations are hugely burdensome: "The traumatized, we might say, carry an impossible history within them, or they become themselves the symptom of a history that they cannot entirely possess." Scholars such as Caruth, Dégh, and MacDonald provide a helpful theoretical framework for understanding accounts of ghosts and hauntings; some African diaspora studies scholars go a step further, specifically employing the motif of death and its associated configurations, including ghosts and hauntings, to theorize about the transatlantic and colonial experience of Africans in the Americas.

In *Lose Your Mother: A Journey along the Atlantic Slave Route*, Saidiya Hartman narrates her tracing of the Atlantic slave trade from Ghana to the Americas. Short notes given to her by some schoolboys outside Elmina Castle suggested that in her status as an American, they considered her a "*kosanba*," or "spirit child."[14] Also known as the "come, go back, child," the *kosanba* shuttles back and forth between the worlds of the living and the dead because of stories not passed on, ancestors not remembered, things lost, and debts not yet paid." According to Hartman, a spirit child "braves the wreckage of history and bears the burden that others refuse." Her study treats this story about death and the ontological instability of the afterlife as a trope. Like Hartman, Ian Baucom follows a discourse related to death. In *Specters of the Atlantic*, he analyzes accounts of the murder of captured Africans jettisoned from the ship *Zong* in 1836, and of the specter produced by those deaths. In relation to the transatlantic slave trade, and to the *Zong* massacre in particular, Baucom hopes to show that "a contemporary black Atlantic allegoresis of the middle passage animates its hauntological interrogation of a classical discourse on justice and exchange."[15] Other African diaspora studies scholars similarly mobilize concepts and metaphors informed by death as a means of critical engagement.

In "Necropolitics," Achille Mbembe uses death and states of disembodiment as a theoretical framework for contemplating sovereignty, advancing the idea that "the ultimate expression of sovereignty resides to a large degree in the power and the capacity to dictate who may live and who must die."[16] Mbembe's definition circumvents traditional understandings of sovereignty as self-dominion and instead locates it more specifically in having control over death. Vincent Brown likewise uses death as an ontological point of entry for his study *The Reaper's Garden: Death and Power in the World of Atlantic Slavery*. He pursues the semantics of death in Jamaica during the era of slavery and asserts that death was Janus-faced, functioning as a binary force that both produced and destroyed.[17] Brown uses the term "mortuary politics" to refer to the negotiations surrounding death, and asserts the basic social importance of death: "Death and its meanings have historically been central to social order and tension. People have derived profound social meaning from the beliefs and practices associated with death, and they have employed those meanings—charged with cosmic importance—in struggles toward particular ends." This importance extends into the realm of future action: "Relations with the dead . . . have the ability to connect private and public concerns, by aligning individual experiences of loss and memory with the interests of community, church, or state. This linkage makes the dead integral to both social organization and political mobilization, and therefore vital to historical transformation." Brown explains that the varying personal and communal histories of the enslaved in the Atlantic world shared similar cosmological views on death: "Most Atlantic Africans recognized a supernatural hierarchy" that included "ancestors and the spirits of the dead."

In *African Religions and Philosophy*, John Mbiti explores religious practices in Africa before colonization.[18] The recently deceased are categorized as the "living dead." He explains that the deceased "of up to five generations" past are in a special state known as the "Sasa period": "These are the 'spirits' with which African people are most concerned" because the living-dead maintain an "interest" in those they left behind. Because of their hybrid status as both human and spirit, they are effective interlocutors between man, God, and the rest of the spirit world. They "warn of impending dangers" and effectively function as "the invisible police of the families and communities" they left behind. The living-dead sustain this vital role in African life until no one with a living memory of that person remains alive. They then transition into the "Zamani period," in which they become "senior" spirits who merge into a communal spirit identity that Mbiti describes as a "state of collective immortality."

Brown claims that in the Atlantic Caribbean, this belief in what Mbiti terms a "state of collective immortality" was sustained: "With these otherworldly beings, most especially with the dead," the enslaved "maintained active relations."[19] He further explains that "from extensive interviews conducted among Africans in the Danish West Indies in 1767–1768, the Moravian missionary Christian George Andreas Oldendorp concluded, 'There is almost no nation in Guinea that does not believe in the immortality of the soul. It is understood by them that the soul continues living after its separation from the body.'"[20] Throughout his text, Brown teases out what he terms the "mortuary politics" informing death practices among the enslaved in Jamaica. For example, funerary rituals allowed the enslaved to experience and restore "a sense of their common humanity." Additionally, the performative nature of the rituals associated with funerals permitted the enslaved to witness their cultural similarities while experiencing their unique communal identity. Other aspects of funerary rituals served important functions such as "defin[ing] familial belongings" and "reinforc[ing] the significance of kinship and friendship."

My methodological approach to the hauntings discussed here is informed by the work of the theorists cited above. If ghost stories are in fact a "barometer of human concerns," as Dégh claims, what are the concerns reflected in the narratives I pursue? Barbara Walker proposes that "if the supernatural is seriously considered, the events and phenomena reported or described within a group give us evidence of a particular way of perceiving the world."[21] This perspective "provides insight into cultural identity" and broadens cultural understanding: "By attending to those patterns, we gather a fuller understanding of what is meaningful to the group, what gives it cohesion and animation." Relying heavily on Brown's ideas in *The Reaper's Garden*, I aim to expose the "mortuary politics" informing the construction of these narratives about death. In Brown's activation of the term, he invokes a "capacious general definition of politics as concerted action toward specific goals."[22] When these oral narratives are read within the context of Caribbean and African cosmologies and funerary rituals, these stories of hauntings reveal what life after death seems to imply about life before death. Additionally, I critically discuss their reproduction in a variety of texts. To be clear, my interest is not to contest or affirm the validity of these duppy narratives. Nonetheless, in the Jamaica in which I grew up, events such as these are believed by many to be entirely possible, and I approach these stories by fully embracing the idea that such seemingly impossible events could indeed occur. What I aim to offer is a critical reading of these stories, since of all the many ghost stories told in Jamaica, they have received a great deal of attention and have come to reside in a place of dominance on the landscape of Jamaican oral narrative.

Hauntings in Jamaica

Probably the most popular Jamaican ghost narrative is the story of Annie Palmer, known as the White Witch of Rose Hall. Palmer's reputed penchant for cruelty to her slaves and her involvement in the occult have further invigorated this ghost story, and its national and international popularity has led to Palmer's former home, the Rose Hall Plantation, becoming a popular tourist destination. This story, however, is not part of this chapter because research indicates it did not emerge from within a community that believed it to be true. Instead, as Laura Lomas explains, "The perseverance of the legend is particularly interesting given that it is thoroughly fabricated, as Geoffrey S. Yates, Glory Robertson and the Jamaica Institute librarians have demonstrated with archival evidence."[23] A pamphlet titled *The Legend of Rose Hall*, reproduced in 1868 in the *Falmouth Post* by John Costello, along with some later articles in the *Jamaica Daily Gleaner*, are among the earliest documents that refer to the Rose Hall legend. These documents help establish that the story about the haunting was generated long after the event occurred and was fabricated with specific narrative objectives in mind.

The three incidents on which this chapter focuses took place in Jamaica during the mid to late twentieth century. When I was a child growing up in Jamaica, these seemed to be the ghost stories that everyone knew, and they remain popular ghost stories in Jamaican lore. I have always found ghost stories compelling—a profound interrogation of what it means to be alive.

Here they provide an opportunity to contemplate how stories circulating within a nationally framed orbit contain insights about the Caribbean, nationally and regionally. In approaching these stories I reject the Western impulse to pathologize ways of knowing unable to easily fit into a conventionally accepted Western epistemological model. Although engaging with the stories in this manner may disrupt Western ways of knowing, I advocate the importance of keeping in mind Caribbean and African approaches to death, the spirit world, and ancestors.

The first paranormal event discussed here involves a set of ghostly encounters that grew out of what is now known as the Kendal train crash. This horrific train accident took place in the Jamaican countryside in 1957 and resulted in the deaths of close to two hundred passengers.[24] To this day, stories prevail about encounters with the wandering spirits of passengers seeking directions or trying to catch buses or taxis to find their way back to their homes. Next is the story of a fugitive coffin on wheels that reportedly navigated its way through Kingston, piloted by three crows perched on top. This incident took place in 1970 and resulted in tremendous panic in and around Kingston. According to newspaper reports, rumors of this event lured thousands of Jamaicans out of schools and offices to line the streets in an effort to catch a glimpse of this bizarre sight.[25] Finally, there is the story of Duppy Shirley, the ghost of a Jamaican immigrant who died abroad in the 1980s but whose spirit returned to Jamaica to haunt family members who owed her money. These stories have lodged themselves so securely in the Jamaican national consciousness that they have been passed to new generations. The hauntings are anchored to specific Jamaican locations, and the events associated with them have been fictionalized in film, fiction, and song.

Kendal Train Crash

The Kendal train crash was a dreadful disaster that occurred on Sunday, September 1, 1957, just before midnight in the small town of Kendal, Manchester, in Jamaica.[26] Hundreds of members of the congregation of St. Anne's Roman Catholic Church had left Kingston early that morning for an excursion to Montego Bay, and on the return trip that night, the train derailed and plunged over a precipice. Approximately two hundred people were killed and another seven hundred injured. Among the dead were members of St.

Anne's as well as numerous alleged thugs who had illicitly boarded the train. The Kendal crash was called "the worst rail disaster in Jamaica's history and the second worst rail disaster in the world at that time." Subsequent investigations determined that the crash was caused by a brake malfunction.

While growing up in Jamaica, I heard numerous recitations of duppy stories involving the Kendal crash. In all the stories, the ghosts of crash victims were trying to get transportation back home. In a 2002 article, Barbara Ellington reports that "stories are still told throughout Manchester about cab drivers who picked up passengers in the months following the crash only to arrive at their destination and discover they had been carrying a 'Kendal crash duppy' who had mysteriously disappeared along the way."[27] According to one account from a personal acquaintance of mine, a woman who lived in Kingston at Laws Street lost her two daughters in the crash.[28] A good while after their death, a taxi picked up a pair of well-dressed girls whose destination was Laws Street. The girls were in good spirits, laughing and talking for the entire journey. When taxi arrived at its destination, the girls asked whether they could go inside to get the money to pay for the trip. The driver agreed, and waited for an extended time, but the girls did not return. He eventually knocked on the door of the house and asked the occupant for the young ladies. The mother, stricken with shock and grief, explained that no one had come into the house and that she had lost her two daughters in the crash.

A similar story is told of a nurse who took a cab from an area near the site of the wreck to her home, not far away. It was late at night and the driver could not see her well, and during the short journey, she did not look him in the face and or say much. Replicating the sequence of just about every other Kendal crash story, when the taxi driver got the nurse to her house, she explained that she had to go inside for money. Because it was dark, the taxi driver did not clearly see her enter the house, but as with the sisters in my acquaintance's story, the nurse never returned. The driver honked his horn, but no one came out. The next morning, he returned to the house, where he was told that several other drivers had had the same experience and that the woman he transported was a nurse who lived in the house before she died. According to occupants of the house, she perished in the crash precisely around the same time of night when the drivers picked her up. Similar

Kendal crash duppy stories abound, and they have been permanently written into the Jamaican ghost-story landscape.

Stories about the Kendal crash duppies, like those of Jamaica's other famous hauntings, have been fictionalized a number of times, including in Beverly East's novel *Reaper of Souls*. Loosely based on the experiences of the author's family, which lost fourteen people in the crash, East's novel traces the sorrowful aftermath of this tragedy on the fictional Scott family, especially three siblings: Austin, Esther, and Eve. Plagued by depression, mental illness, and the trauma of relocating to England, the Scott family must come to terms with the tragic unfolding of what was meant to be an enjoyable family outing. Characters in the novel acknowledge the proliferation of duppy stories that erupt in relation to the crash. Esther explains: "Stories of ghosts and strange occurrences surfaced everywhere and every person somehow seemed to know at least one . . . In the most popular the dead and missing were showing up in bedrooms and on balconies, floating about and banging on doors."[29] There ends up, of course, being just such a ghostly encounter in the novel, and it involves a cousin, Donovan, a crash survivor living in the Scott family house.

Donovan has a torrid relationship with an intriguing woman named Lucy, who "had skin that was soft and ochre like olive oil. She wore a lost look on her face. Her deepest grey eyes stared at you as if she had seen the world four times over."[30] Not only is Lucy's countenance strange, but her dress is also quite unusual, and the jingling sound she makes suggests her otherworldliness: "From head to toe, she was decorated in jewelry. Beads and more than one crucifix hung around her neck: three clip-on earrings hung from her ear lobes, every finger including her thumbs had more than one ring on them. With every move she made, she jingled." Donovan's cousin Esther and the family housekeeper eventually realize that Lucy's shoes look a lot like those that Esther's mother was wearing when she died at Kendal. Given reports that rampant looting occurred at the crash site, Esther begins to wonder whether Lucy was among those thieves who stole from the victims. When she tells Donovan and he confronts Lucy about it, her response is unusual: "The smug smile she wore evaporated from her face. She promptly stood up straight, stepped out of the shoes, peeled off every item of jewelry, the rings, the bangles, the necklaces, brooches, pins, earrings and rings from all parts of her body and placed them beside the shoes. Without saying another word, Lucy left the house in her bare feet." Lucy never returns to the house, and after some time passes, Donovan goes looking for her at the library where she said she worked. The librarian explains that no one there has ever seen or heard of a Lucy, and that she is not an employee of the library. Bewildered, Donovan begins to leave, but on his way out spots a poster with photographs of people who are missing and presumed dead from the crash. Mysteriously beckoned by the poster, Donovan wanders over and sees a photo of his beloved Lucy staring back at him with her grey eyes.

Lucy's deep desire for corporeality is seen in her excessive attention to the adornment of her body. She so badly wants to be "real" that she festoons herself with accessories in a futile effort to overcome her disembodiment. A similar desperation to resume a state of embodiment is reflected in all the oral histories about Kendal crash duppies who caught cabs or bummed rides; like Lucy, they all eventually end up revealed as ghosts. These stories speak to a collective national desire that the deceased could make their way back home to their loved ones and that life could resume as it was before. Each iteration of a Kendal crash story and the disruption enacted by the encounter resulted in a halting reminder that the crash occurred and that lives were disrupted.

In *Myth and Meaning*, Claude Lévi-Strauss defines the term "explanatory cell," which is a way to understand the evolution of myths that may maintain the same "structure" with different "content." Lévi-Strauss uses the example of different iterations of a myth about a conflict that resulted in the destruction of a town. Versions of this myth say that a conflict arose because "a husband killed the lover of his wife, or that the brothers killed their sister's lover, or that a husband killed his wife because she had a lover." Although the details of each story differ, the essence remains the same: romance led to murder. One can argue that the variations in stories about the Kendal crash can be accounted for similarly, and our attention needs to be directed to the place where the versions of these narratives are imbricated. In this case, that locus seems to be an effort to connect with family and perhaps even provide assurance of well-being through a demonstration of disembodied existence.

The Kendal tragedy captured global attention because it was one of the world's worse train wrecks at that time. The gory visibility of the body parts and the bodies was captured by newspaper photographers and witnessed by many who flocked to the scene of the accident, which certainly added to the horror of the nation's experience of the tragedy.[31] Even now, many older Jamaicans who were alive at the time of the crash claim knowledge of families that lost someone in the crash or, as in the novel, lost multiple family members. Furthermore, numerous children perished in the crash, augmenting the associated sense of tragedy. Because the names and ages of the dead were printed in the newspaper in the days that followed, the entire country in many ways bore witness to each death.[32]

The belief that life endures beyond death has been a persistent feature of Caribbean spirituality. Vincent Brown explains that even after the adoption of Christianity among slaves in Jamaica, they maintained a belief in the coexistence of spirits on the earthly plane.[33] Likewise, "many Africans" thought that the soul of the departed "lingered, sometimes ominously, around its dead body or homestead." The nine-night ritual practiced in parts of the Caribbean affirms this belief and acknowledges the days before the ninth night after death as the transition period for the spirit of the deceased. The nine-night interval thus becomes an opportunity for friends and family to say a final good-bye to the deceased. An account of a nine-night ceremony in 1953 in Jamaica indicates that at midnight, the spirit of the deceased is expected to speak through someone present at the ceremony, communicating information such as how to manage the belongings of the deceased, the cause of death, or a forewarning to family members of impending danger.[34] The reports of Kendal crash duppies acknowledge the widespread belief in individual agency that can survive a state of disembodiment.

Aside from the massive scope of the island's loss of life, newspaper stories following up on the Kendal crash in September 1957 provide additional insight into that historical moment. Articles bemoaned the "hooliganism" of illicit riders on the excursion and celebrated the presumed death of a notorious criminal named Spliff in the crash.[35] The *Kingston Daily Gleaner* also mentioned the anticipated arrival of railway investigative experts from Britain to figure out what had happened, and announced an increase in the lending rate from the Bank of England, which the minister of finance, Noel Nethersole, described as "shattering" to the Jamaican economy. These reports indicate two important aspects of Jamaican sociopolitical life at that time: an increasing fear of lawlessness and criminal behavior, and increasing discomfort with Jamaica's dependence on Britain.

Maybe these anxieties, coupled with an inability to fully absorb the tragedy, in many ways informed the nature of the duppy stories that caught the nation's attention at the time of the crash. Perhaps the shaping of the Kendal crash duppies as presences unwilling to accept their destinies signaled a national desire to resist both the tragedy and Jamaica's worsening social, political, and economic conflicts. These issues, which had grown much worse a decade later, were foreshadowed by the country's dependence on foreign resources and its growing social deterioration, marked by the perception of an increase in "hooliganism" and general criminal activity. Additionally, at the time of the crash, the promise of Jamaica's independence from Great Britain was brewing (it would take place only five years later, in 1962). Perhaps some of the outcries about hooligans and moral decline might have anticipated the end of British rule and reflected fears about the country's ability to assume independent nationhood and protect its citizens.

A Bird-Driven Coffin in Kingston

In 1970, a peculiar occurrence was reported that again caught the attention of the entire island. This incident, which was not a national tragedy, involved the surprising sighting of a coffin navigating its way across the island, steered by three John crows (turkey vultures) perched on top and dressed in suits. This incident so fascinated the nation that newspaper reporters were sent to cover the story. An article titled "Hundreds Seek the Coffin and Crows" was published in the *Daily Gleaner* the day after the incident. It explains that on the previous day, thousands of Jamaicans abandoned whatever they were doing and poured into the streets of Kingston and Spanish Town to catch a view of the renegade coffin and its three pilots. According to the report, "Witnesses professed seeing the unguided coffin at various points in the Corporate Area. Some claimed that it only appeared to the eye at infrequent intervals."[36]

The report offers the following description of the incident by a young woman who provided an official account to the police: "It had three wheels and looked like a man-sized coffin. It was brown in front and black on the back. There were three John crows perched on top of it—two big-sized ones and a little one."[37] The witness added that two of the John crows wore black coats and one red. When the coffin stopped at the Peter Claver Primary School in Kingston, she observed the crow in the red coat ask a teacher whether she knew someone named John Brown. According to the young woman making the report, the teacher fainted. According to the newspaper article, another witness corroborated the young woman's story; however, the principal at the school denied that any such thing took place. There were claims of sightings of the coffin not only in downtown Kingston and in Spanish Town, but also in other parts of the island. The story of the three crows steering a coffin has remained a popular story about the Jamaican spectacular.

The John crow is a figure heavily invested with symbolic meaning in Jamaica and indeed throughout the African diaspora.[38] The John crow, more specifically identified as a turkey vulture or a turkey buzzard, is well known among Jamaicans as both a literal and a symbolic signifier of death.[39] A carrion bird, its physical presence communicates that a death has occurred; furthermore, the bird is often considered a bad omen. Constructed as representing death, blackness, and what Jamaicans would call "bad minded" behavior (which refers to any action inspired by questionable intentions), the John crow appears in a number of popular Jamaican sayings:

- "You favor John crow" (You look like a John crow). This means you are ugly in any number of ways, including because of your black racial heritage.
- "Every John crow think him pickney white" (Every John crow believes his child is white). This means people always believe (erroneously) that their children are better than them.
- "If you fly with John crow, you will nyam (eat) dead meat." This just reiterates the distasteful habits associated with the John crow and suggests that keeping unsavory company will lead one to engage in unsavory behavior.

These sayings are among several that regularly circulate among Jamaicans and sustain the idea of the John crow as a repulsive outlier existing on the margins of civilized society. The foulness associated with the John crow is expressed in the use of the term as a naming mechanism for anything strong or vile. For example, Jamaican overproof rum (typically, higher than 114 proof) is commonly referred to as John crow batty (butt) because it is very strong and potent. Additionally, the bladder of a cow is also known as a John crow nose.

The John crow is also referred to in a number of Jamaican songs, and knowledge of the incident involving the coffin is so common that the Jamaican reggae artist Bob Marley wrote and recorded as song about it. In Bob Marley's song "Mr. Brown," the narrator repeatedly queries the literal and symbolic identity of the elusive Mr. Brown, the catalyst for the crows' quest: "Who is Mr. Brown? Mr. Brown is a clown who rides through town in a coffin / Where he be found?"[40] Marley also situates Mr. Brown as an agent of chaos when he sings about the real-life turmoil that erupted in the downtown area of Kingston known as Parade when rumors of the traveling coffin spread: "From Mandeville to Sligoville, coffin running around / Upsetting, upsetting, upsetting the town / Asking for Mr. Brown." According to a newspaper report, the crowd that gathered at the time of the sighting was so unruly that businesses in the area had to close for fear of rioting, and traffic came to a halt.[41]

The song describes the crows as "chauffeur-driven," a term that Marley uses tongue in cheek, highlighting the somewhat carnivalesque element of the sightings. These lines hint at an apparent disruption in the social hierarchy and suggest that the crows represent Jamaica's working class, since the crows, marginal figures, surprisingly have a chauffeur. Additionally, Marley positions the coffin-piloting birds as deceptive trickster figures who are simply pretending to not know the missing Mr. Brown: "What a thing in town / Crows, chauffeur driven around / Skankin as if they had never known / the man they call Mr. Brown." This view of the birds as tricksters is enhanced by Marley's use of the term "skankin" to describe their activity. In Jamaican parlance, this term means something like "skulking" and connotes a suspicious activity. This construction of the crows in Marley's song as a referent for Jamaica's marginalized poor evokes a possible reading of the hysteria over this sighting as symptomatic of the island's growing anxieties regarding crime and the country's restless, underemployed population.

Caribbean funerary rituals provide another point of entry for analysis of the story of the wayward coffin. In *Obeah: Witchcraft in the West Indies* (1883), written by Hesketh Bell, who served in the British Foreign Service, is a description of a funeral in Grenada, where he was stationed for part of his career. Bell explains that "the coffin striking against anything in its progress is taken as a very evil sign by the bearers."[42] In *Black Roadways: A Study of Jamaican Folk Life* (1929), written by the American ethnographer and folklorist Martha Beckwith, the author describes a divination process in Jamaica in which the coffin takes on agency. Beckwith reports an instance in which a man did not want to be buried at a certain location, and so the coffin holding him became extra heavy, slowing down its progress.[43] Vincent Brown explains that in the Caribbean world, "as pallbearers carried the body, laid upon an open bier or—less frequently—in a coffin, they became mediums for the departing spirit."[44] In this role as interlocutors for the deceased, pallbearers would, as guided, stop at houses in the community to "demand reparations and atonement from debtors and enemies." In an account by James Phillippo, a nineteenth-century Baptist missionary in Jamaica, pallbearers "would sometimes make a sudden halt, put their ears in a listening attitude against the coffin, pretending that the corpse was endowed with the gift of speech—that he was angry and required to be appeased, gave instructions for a different distribution of his property, objected to his mode of conveyance, or refused to proceed farther towards the place of burial until some debts due to him were discharge, some slanderous imputation on his character removed, some theft confessed."[45] This praxis of "supernatural inquest,"[46] with roots in Africa, has readily apparent implications for the haunted coffin maneuvering through Kingston, engaged in a dialogue with the crows serving as pallbearer-mediums. Perhaps in their symbolic representation of Jamaica's black working class, the crows register the economic and social injustices experienced by that population and assert that atonement must be made. That the coffin was reportedly seen in many locations suggests that the responsibility for the challenges faced by working-class Jamaicans at the time was a communal one.

While newspaper accounts of the incident and Marley's song characterize the crows as saying very few words, I suggest that their embodied disposition serves as part of their divination narrative. The racially loaded image of the John crow is not uncommon in Jamaican culture.[47] For example, the Jamaican folksong "John Crow Say Him Nah Work Pon Sunday" (John Crow says he doesn't work on Sundays) alludes to the historically repressive labor practices that working-class black Jamaicans have had to endure. Even the Jamaican nomenclature used in reference to albino John crows, whose plumage is mostly white, shows how heavily imbued the bird is with notions of race. An albino John crow is called a headman John crow, a King crow, or a John crow parson; it is the bird "to which the black John crows defer."[48] The privilege unlocked by the albino John crow's whiteness is reflected in its names, which evoke slavery and the types of subjects given privilege within the colonial project.

The folk song "Wheel and Turn Me" also suggests that subjects like the John crow—black subjects—are not only less desirable as sexual partners but also potentially malicious and destructive. The song tells the story of a woman who purchases fancy new clothes with money she received from a suitor. She has washed these clothes and set them out on a bush to dry when "one ole un-conscionable John crow" swoops down and swipes her clothing, threatening to soil and damage the new outfits and, ostensibly, the woman's prospects for keeping her new beau. The verse that follows is a plea to the interfering and malicious John crow to not damage her clothing (and her reputation): "No tear it Jeremiah, no tear it / No tear up me silk an' satin."[49] A later verse pleads "A why you deh wheel and turn me / You must want me fe go fall down / And lick my belly pon tambourina" (Why are you wheeling and turning me / You must want me to fall / And hit my belly on a tambourine). The John crow is situated as "bad minded" through his tormenting of the narrator. Furthermore, the song suggest that the John crow (Jeremiah) is sexually undesirable and has set out to "ruin" the woman's reputation and prospects with her suitor through violently forcing himself on her. Her concern about falling (from grace) and hitting her belly on a tambourine certainly signals the potential disgrace of unwed pregnancy and the resounding scandal it would create for the woman.

The racializing of the John crow is evident in a variety of cultural artifacts. Anna Kasafi Perkins argues, "How we have loaded down the poor John crow is an indication that the race question is alive and well among Jamaicans of a new generation albeit in a different fashion."[50] She identifies the John crow not only as a racial signifier but also as a "sentinel" that reflects the "the psychological health of the Jamaican society." Interestingly, the John crow has long been revered as an intermediary with the spiritual realm. Among the Yoruba of West Africa, Adewale Owoseni and Isaac Olufemi Olatoye explain that the vulture "is a sacred bird and should not be used as a burnt offering, game or food."[51] Evidence for this is seen in a Yoruban proverb: "We do not kill the vulture, we do not eat the vulture, we do not use the vulture as sacrifice to the gods to remedy human destiny."

In an article titled "Plants, Spirits, and the Meaning of 'John' in Jamaica," John Rashford suggests that phrases containing the name "John" have a "relationship to the world of spirits and spirit possession."[52] Rashford gives several examples, including "John Canoe," whom he describes as "the chief dancer of a troupe of dancers ... a spirit person or Obeah-man"; and "John Crow Bead," a seed used to make "amulets and charms." The name John Crow itself "could be taken to mean Obeah-man's, sorcerer's, or magician's crow." The John crow's role as a literal signifier of death is well known among Jamaicans, since a carrion bird eats the carcasses of dead animals. But as Rashford explains, in its capacity as a connection to the spirit world, it is also "an omen of death," and its presence creates great concern. Additionally, Martha Beckwith notes that crows flying at sunset are portentous and symbolize a "funeral procession."[53] Perkins relates the story of a John crow that turned up in the office of the principal at a Jamaican school in 2012. The story was reported in the newspaper, and an important feature of the description is the avalanche of prayers for protection that ensued as efforts were made to remove the crow by school staff.[54] This response was anchored in the crow's presumed role as a sentinel of death and suffering.

The year 1970, when the sighting of the coffins occurred, marked the close of a turbulent decade for Jamaica. Anthony Payne explains that "During the 1960s some of the strains long contained by the Jamaican political system began to emerge more into the open."[55] Although the island had seemingly met economic growth milestones during the 1960s, the economic situation was in fact worsening, according to Payne: "Income distribution was more uneven than ever, the share of the poorest 40 per cent of the population in personal earned income declining from 7.2 per cent in 1958 to 5.4 per cent in 1968. Illiteracy, poor housing, and unemployment remained the lot of vast numbers of Jamaicans. Indeed, the level of unemployment and underemployment in the society had increased hugely, doubling from 12 per cent to 24 per cent during the very period of fast economic growth." The 1960s in Jamaica were also marked by a series of violent political uprisings, including the Henry "rebellion," an attempt to overthrow the government in 1960; the Coral Gardens incident in 1963, a state-sanctioned attack on a Rastafarian community arising from a land dispute; the anti-Chinese riots in 1965, resulting from allegations that a woman was beaten by her Chinese employer; election-related violence from 1966 to 1967; and in 1968 what became known as the Rodney riots. These riots ensued after a University of the West Indies (UWI) history lecturer, Dr. Walter Rodney, was banned from returning to the island to his position at the Mona campus. UWI students led the demonstration, which, Payne explains, "spilled over into an outbreak of rioting and looting on the part of the unemployed, urban poor and *lumpenproletariat* of Kingston." The worsening economic conditions and the social unrest collaborated to create a milieu that must have been a source of tremendous exasperation, particularly for the poorest Jamaicans as they tried to make economic headway. The surge in crime and the vulnerability of Jamaican citizens to it, regardless of wealth or fame, was perhaps most strikingly seen in the attempted murder of the island's beloved reggae ambassador, Bob Marley, in 1976; he fled Jamaica for several years after the attempt on his life. The crows roaming through town on top of a coffin were certainly an ominous image, and I suggest that this now-iconic image of the crows embodies national anxieties about the social unrest of the 1960s and the dissatisfaction that was breaking out across the island by 1970.

Duppy Shirley

The third haunting on which this essay focuses sustains the attention to class reflected in the story of the crows. The haunting, which gained national attention in Jamaica during the 1980s, features the disgruntled ghost of a Jamaican woman named Shirley. She passed away while living overseas, and rumor was that Shirley had lent money to family in Jamaica, and upon her death, her repatriated ghost hounded her debtors for repayment. At the time of the incident, one of the dominant activities in stories of the haunting involved the pelting of Shirley's family's roof with stones, along with the general terrorizing of a home where several of Shirley's indebted associates lived. This haunting became the subject of widespread discussion, and even television news reports. Shirley's story was subsequently retold in song and in film. The single "Shirley Duppy," by Junie Ranks, recounts the haunting, explaining that Shirley returned to the island from overseas to collect money owed to her by family members.[56] The song offers specifies acts of antagonism performed by Shirley's ghost, including throwing stones, setting fires, and physically attacking some victims.[57] Additionally, the song's refrain, which states that it is not Shirley who owes her victims but her victims who owe Shirley, draws attention to the economic vulnerability of the people being molested by Shirley's duppy and their state of dependency.

The film *Shirley Duppy*, an amateur but intriguing undertaking, offers a similar but more elaborately fictionalized version of the haunting.[58] It is set in a poor inner-city community that is being tormented by the ghost of a woman known to the community as Miss Shirley. She died while living overseas and has returned to collect money from those in the community who owe her. For a good deal of the film, Shirley's ghost is whipping up a gust of wind, bellowing in a deep and eerie voice, or startling someone with a slap across the face. Several members of the community are so alarmed that they begin to gather money to place in her grave, and the main character, Kisko, terrified to his wit's end, decides to consult an Obeah man for help. The Obeah man gives him some specially prepared water to pour into the grave to end the hauntings, but while Kisko is digging up Miss Shirley's grave, he realizes that the money is in there that other folks have left, and he decides to steal it. The film ends with Kisko being violently attacked by Miss Shirley's ghost, upset over this attempt to pilfer her money. At numerous points in the film, a scene cuts to a shot of a plane flying overhead, which seems intended to be an ominous reminder of Miss Shirley's presence on the island from overseas, but the planes may be read as markers of another kind of foreign presence associated with Jamaica's economic challenges.

The film *Shirley Duppy* focuses on a phenomenon long familiar in the Caribbean community: immigrants to metropoles sending remittances back home, often as gifts and sometimes as loans to assist family and friends with everything from building houses to buying school uniforms. The people who end up being terrorized by Shirley have borrowed her hard-earned money and not repaid it, and it is for this infraction that they end up being haunted. As I contemplate this haunting, trying to make sense of why it received so much attention, I cannot help considering the economic parallels between Shirley's borrowers and the island itself. This haunting, which occurred in the early 1980s amidst Jamaica's exploding economic and social crises, showcases the plight faced by the Jamaican government, which borrowed extensively from the IMF and endured the terror of that institution's fiscal haunting. This haunting of Jamaica's economic landscape primarily took the form of structural adjustment policies required by the IMF and the World Bank in return for the nation's access to loans. The 1980s began on a very grim note, and according to Abbie Bakan, "the average income in Jamaica was 25 percent lower and the cost of living 320 percent higher" than they were eight years earlier.[59]

In *Haunting Experiences*, Jeannie Thomas recounts a similar ghost story from Cape Breton Island, in Canada. In this story, a clergyman experienced a visitation by his recently deceased father.[60] The father indicated that he had an outstanding bill with a merchant, but the son was doubtful about this, since he had paid all his father's debt after his passing. Struck by the encounter, the son contacted the proprietor, who initially insisted no money was owed, but after checking more carefully, it turned out the deceased father did owe for a bill from twenty-five years prior for precisely the amount the spirit had indicated during its visit. The son paid the quarter-century-old bill. Thomas argues that because of the importance of credit in the "poor economy" where the visit from the dad occurred, the story highlights the communal anxieties about debt and reinforces "the cultural value that debts should be paid."

The divination component of funerary rituals in Jamaica often aims at ensuring that unpaid debts were discharged. Beckwith refers to the "habit of collecting bad debts on the way to the grave," and explains that if pallbearers are guided to stop at someone's house, indicating that someone there did an injustice to the deceased, "such a one must pay the corpse before it moves on."[61] Though a coffin is not involved in the haunting by Shirley's duppy, this visitation functions in much the same as the divination of a coffin did in the Atlantic Caribbean, where, Vincent Brown explains, "offenses that had been committed against the deceased had to be atoned for before the spirit could leave the community."[62] Brown adds that "the threat of spectral revenge was supposed to be the severest moral sanction against thieves, debtors, and witches." In *The Sun and the Drum*, Leonard Barrett explains that a duppy must be "satisfied that the living have done their duty toward the dead," or it may (like Duppy Shirley) "become angry, vindictive, and otherwise troublesome."[63] Beckwith explains that duppies reportedly have a great propensity to commit harm, including throwing stones, physical assault, and arson.[64] Furthermore, the revenge that Duppy Shirley wrought on her community was similar to the insistence of the corpses that Brown describes, pressing for justice. And while Duppy Shirley had personal debts to collect from her community, her narrative of disembodiment suggests that her haunting of the community spoke to a more expansive financial haunting simultaneously taking place on the national landscape.

According to *The Encyclopedia of the Nations*, Jamaica in the early 1980s borrowed extensively: "[In] 1981, Jamaica became the number-one per capita recipient of IMF lending in the world. Jamaica also received extensive funding from the World Bank, ranking as the number-one per capita recipient in 1982."[65] The best-known and, some would argue, most damaging of the structural adjustment policies put in place as a condition of the loans was the required devaluation of Jamaica's currency. In the era leading up to the 1980s, the value of Jamaicans' cash holdings plummeted while the cost of everything went up. There was a massive flight of capital and citizens, who fled as fast as if a duppy were in pursuit.

Stories about both Duppy Shirley and the three John crows speak to the acute socioeconomic anxieties that swelled over the course of the 1960s and 1970s. Using Caribbean funerary rituals as a theoretical lens exposes how these modern ghost narratives are haunted by the memory of slavery and the colonial encounter. Just as African-derived rituals and beliefs associated with death asserted the agency and personhood of deceased slaves in ways the colonial machinery resisted acknowledging, these ghost stories emphasize the concerns and aspirations of the embodied and often disenfranchised by drawing attention to the agency of the disembodied. These fantastical narratives continue the work of funerary rituals, and Brown contends that "as the focus of community memory, the dead had enormous power to enforce communal values."[66] He adds that based on the opportunities the spirit of the dead had "to accuse or to convey its own moral essence, the funeral also provided an occasion for social persuasion." The ghost stories I discuss offer similar opportunities and provide commentary on the plight the nation. The introduction to *Haunting Experiences* suggests that bottle trees, popular in the American South and the Caribbean as a mechanism for capturing evil spirits, function as an apt symbolic representation of the function of ghost stories, which encapsulate communal fears about aspects of life.[67]

CHAPTER FOUR

Exodus

*The Intergalactic Movement of Jah People
in the Works of Tobias Buckell*

> What more sci-fi than Santo Domingo?
> What more fantasy than the Antilles?
> JUNOT DÍAZ

In *Billion Year Spree: The True History of Science Fiction*, Brian W. Aldiss touts Mary Shelley's *Frankenstein* as the first science fiction (sci-fi) novel, though not all critics agree with him.[1] *Frankenstein*, first published in 1818, is the well-known tale of a nameless and much reviled "monster," and the novel is freighted with issues relating to class, race, and the politics of embodiment. Only a few decades after *Frankenstein* appeared came the publication of what might be the first Anglophone Caribbean sci-fi novel, and it also is a contemplation of class, race, and embodiment. *Emmanuel Appadocca; or, Blighted Life: A Tale of the Boucaneers*, written by the Trinidadian Maxwell Philip, was published in 1854.[2] Described on the cover of the 1997 edition of the novel as "the story of a mulatto son's quest for vengeance against his white father, a sugar planter, who abandoned him and his mother," *Emmanuel Appadocca* is a swashbuckling work filled with pirates and swift pursuits on the high seas.

The novel features a pirate ship, the *Black Schooner*, which is central to the plot. It is situated as a liminal, shape-shifting entity that resembles a "large serpent" and is at times imperceptible to other crafts approaching from the distance.[3] Moving between ship and animal, the real and the fantastical, the *Black Schooner* repeatedly evades the Royal Navy by periodically rendering itself invisible or disguising itself as a different vessel. The *Black Schooner*'s transformative ability is engineered through the ship's rigging mechanism, but this technology does not entirely account for the ship's almost instantaneous transformation, which suggests that it has other mysterious abilities: "The Black Schooner sprang forth as she felt the power of her snow-white sails, which, with the rapidity of lightning, had now clothed her tall masts. This metamorphosis was so sudden, that the schooner had already begun to move before the boatmen comprehended the change." *Emmanuel Appadocca*, then, marks a fledgling effort toward rendering a literary-fantastical articulation of the region.

This chapter jumps a century and a half after *Emmanuel Appadocca* was published to explore the ongoing emergence of contemporary Anglophone Caribbean science fiction. I begin by surveying some of the developing theoretical approaches to science fiction in postcolonial and African diaspora studies. Additionally, I explore the work of the Caribbean sci-fi writer Tobias Buckell and consider how he constructs the Caribbean and its citizens in a genre that is identified by its affiliation with the uncanny. Specifically, I discuss his first three novels, *Crystal Rain* (2006), *Ragamuffin* (2007), and *Sly Mongoose* (2008), part of his Xenowealth series.

Within the field of Anglophone Caribbean literary studies, Nalo Hopkinson is perhaps the best-known and most broadly studied sci-fi writer. Indeed, only a few Caribbean writers are recognized as falling squarely in the sci-fi genre. In addition to Hopkinson, who is of Jamaican and Guyanese parentage, and Buckell, who was born in Grenada, other Anglophone Caribbean sci-fi writers include, Karen Lord (Barbados), Stephanie Saulter (Jamaica), and R. S. A. Garcia (Trinidad and Tobago). These writers are increasingly attracting global critical attention, along with their contemporaries in other parts of the Caribbean such as Cuba's José Miguel Sánchez Gómez, who writes under the pen name Yoss.

Buckell, Hopkinson, Lord, and all the emerging Caribbean sci-fi writers are heirs to a rich legacy of fantastical Caribbean narratives from across the region, The ghostly flute in Edgar Mittelholzer's *My Bones and My Flute* (1955); Derek Walcott's *Omeros* (1990), which situates Ma Kilman's fat body as a source of supernatural abundance; the mysterious men known as *mentohs* in Patrick Chamoiseau's *Texaco* (1992); Marlon James's duppy narrator in *A Brief History of Seven Killings* (2014); and the cloven-hoofed Rebekah in

Tiphanie Yanique's *The Land of Love and Drowning* (2014) are just a few examples of Caribbean literature that spotlight the fantastic.

Furthermore, the work of contemporary Caribbean sci-fi writers is in conversation with their African American sci-fi predecessors such as Samuel Delaney and Octavia Butler. In fact, the collections *Dark Matter: A Century of Speculative Fiction from the African Diaspora* (2000), edited by Sheree R. Thomas, and *Whispers from the Cotton Tree Root: Caribbean Fabulist Fiction* (2000), edited by Nalo Hopkinson, feature science fiction as well as essays about the genre from across the African New World. Both of these anthologies announced the diaspora's claim to the genre.

An ongoing debate in the world of sci-fi scholarship is the definition of the genre's name. The fiction produced by some of the writers in the anthologies mentioned above is identified as speculative, fabulist, fantastical, or magical realist, among other descriptors. Perhaps the most enduring definition of sci-fi, and the one used in this chapter, comes from Darko Suvin, who, in his 1972 essay "On the Poetics of the Science Fiction Genre," defines sci-fi as "a literary genre whose necessary and sufficient conditions are the presence and interaction of estrangement and cognition, and whose main formal device is an imaginative framework alternative to the author's empirical environment."[4] Suvin's description essentially proposes that sci-fi involves an encounter with the uncanny—the experience of coming across something known yet unfamiliar in a surrogate landscape constructed on the foundation of current imaginings about unrealized possibilities.

It strikes me that Suvin's often-cited description of the genre sounds a lot like Africans' experience of transatlantic slavery. The European slavers, with their strange tongues, unusual dress, and pale skin, were unlike anything the Africans had seen, but were nevertheless recognizable as human. Additionally, the starkly different geographic and cultural spaces these Africans encountered in the New World could count as "alternative" landscapes, and from the perspective of the enslaved Africans, the landscapes were no doubt "imaginative." In fact, taking this sci-fi motif further, the Middle Passage could be considered the original alien-abduction tale—one is captured by strange creatures from another world, put on their ship, and taken to an entirely new geographic and cultural space in a world one did not even know existed. This association of the New World with the fantastic has a long history, from Columbus's letter to Luis de Santangel, in which he describes

Hispaniola as "a marvel," to Alejo Carpentier's essay "On the Marvelous Real in America," in which he writes, "After all, what is the entire history of America if not a chronicle of the marvelous real?"[5]

Mark Dery proposes that African Americans—and I would include all New World Africans—"in a very real sense, are the descendants of alien abductees; they inhabit a sci-fi nightmare in which unseen but no less impassable force fields of intolerance frustrate their movements: official histories undo what has been done; and technology is too often brought to bear on black bodies."[6] As examples of this kind of technology, Dery cites "branding" and "forced sterilization." One of the best-known accounts of such an abduction is found in *The Interesting Narrative of the Life of Olaudah Equiano* (1789). It and *The Brief Wondrous Life of Oscar Wao* both feature protagonists whose lives are significantly informed and transformed by their encounter with the Caribbean, and both texts assert the fantastical nature of this encounter.

Born an Ibo in 1745 in the village of Isseke, Nigeria, Olaudah Equiano was abducted by slave traders at age eleven.[7] Taken at first to Barbados, shortly after his arrival in the West Indies, Equiano was sold to an officer in the Royal Navy and eventually to a Quaker in Montserrat. After spending ten years in slavery, he was able to earn his freedom, and in 1789 he published his autobiography. Equiano describes his abduction as an intensely traumatic event, not unlike contemporary urban legends about alien abductions: "One day, when all our people were gone out to their works as usual, and I and my dear sister were left to mind the house, two men and a woman got over our walls, and in a moment seized us both, and without giving us time to cry out, or make resistance, they stopped our mouths, and ran off with us into the nearest wood."

After an arduous journey, Equiano reaches the African coast, where he has the traumatic experience of being forced onto a slave ship. Of his initial encounter with the sea and the ship, he writes:

> The first object which saluted my eyes when I arrived on the coast, was the sea, and a slave ship, which was then riding at anchor, and waiting for its cargo. These filled me with astonishment, which was soon converted into terror, when I was carried on board. I was immediately handled and tossed up to see if I were sound, by some of the crew; and I was now per-

suaded that I had gotten into a world of bad spirits, and that they were going to kill me. Their complexions, too, differing so much from ours, their long hair, and the language they spoke (which was very different from any I had ever head), united to confirm me in this belief. Indeed, such were the horrors of my views and fears at the moment, that, if ten thousand worlds had been my own, I would have freely parted with them all to have exchanged my condition with that of the meanest slave in my own county. When I looked round the ship too, and saw a large furnace of copper boiling, and a multitude of black people of every description chained together, every one of their countenances expressing dejection and sorrow, I no longer doubted of my fate; and, quite overpowered with horror and anguish, I fell motionless on the deck and fainted.

Kodwo Eshun suggests that the American Nobel laureate Toni Morrison offers a related approach for theorizing the African presence in the Americas: "Toni Morrison argued that the African subjects that experienced capture, theft, abduction, mutilation, and slavery were the first moderns. They underwent real conditions of existential homelessness, alienation, dislocation, and dehumanization that philosophers like Nietzsche would later define as quintessentially modern. Instead of civilizing African subjects, the forced dislocation and commodification that constituted the Middle Passage meant that modernity was rendered forever suspect."[8]

These implicit connections between the shaping of the New World and sci-fi would perhaps lead one to assume that Caribbean and other postcolonial-identified writers would be drawn to the sci-fi genre in droves, but this has not been the case. In the introduction to the anthology *So Long Been Dreaming: Postcolonial Science Fiction and Fantasy*, Nalo Hopkinson observes the irony that sci-fi "speaks so much about the experience of being alienated, but contains so little written by alienated people themselves."[9] Elisabeth Leonard furthers this contemplation of race and sci-fi: "By far the majority of sf deals with racial tension by ignoring it. In many books the character's race is either not mentioned and probably assumed to be white or, if mentioned, is irrelevant to the events of the story."[10] In her essay "The Future May Be Bleak, But It's Not Black," Thulani Davis too reflects on the portrayal of race, specifically blackness, in sci-fi and asserts that sci-fi renders the African diaspora physiologically and culturally invisible, noting the blankness of black sci-fi characters: "[They have] no family, old school buddies, hometowns, or Harlems. They do not play the dozens . . . They never have dates, or listen to James Brown or even Miles Davis."[11]

Despite this historical displacement of African diasporic characters in sci-fi, De Witt Kilgore suggests that "African Americans must participate in and contest those parts of American culture to which we are not supposed to belong."[12] He notes that "the 'conquest of space' and its promise of a bright future was a crucial component of the American dream." And while Kilgore's assertion might not represent the national aspirations of Caribbean writers, travel to outer space has certainly become a global trope for intellectual and technological advancement, and even those of us who are not rocket scientists know that.

While a variety of scholars have speculated about the interplay of science fiction, race, and the European colonial project, none of these theorists focus specifically on the Caribbean, so the references that follow suggest approaches that use a lens from postcolonial studies or African American studies. Critics such as Istvan Csicsery-Ronay and John Rieder suggest that colonialism and science fiction are intimately connected. Csicsery-Ronay argues, "The dominant sf nations are precisely those that attempted to expand beyond their national borders in imperialist projects," and he views science fiction as "an expression of the political-cultural transformation that originated in European imperialism and was inspired by the ideal of a single global technological regime."[13] Rieder claims that "no informed reader can doubt that allusions to colonial history and situations are ubiquitous features of early science fiction motifs and plots."[14] Rieder further contends that "it is not a matter of asking whether but of determining precisely how and to what extent the stories engage colonialism."

The theorist Isiah Lavender III recognizes the implicit connections between race (and, inevitably, colonialism) and the fantastic. He believes not only that race can be used to analyze science fiction, but also that science fiction traffics in race. He explains that "American sf is characterized by an investment in the proliferation of racial difference, that racial alterity is a fundamental part of sf's narrative and social strategies."[15] Publications by other participants in these conversations about race and space include Jessica Langer's *Postcolonialism and Science Fiction* (2011), Ralph Prozik's *The Quest for Postcolonial Utopia* (2001), Ericka Hoagland and Reema Sarwan's *Science*

Fiction, Imperialism, and the Third World (2010), and Eric Smith's significant intervention in this conversation: *Globalization, Utopia, and Postcolonial Science Fiction* (2012). Smith contends that postcolonial science fiction is particularly poised to unearth "the deep, material interdependencies" between "the first world and the third."[16]

Some sci-fi theorists labor under the umbrella of "Afrofuturism" studies. The cultural critic Mark Dery, who coined the term, uses it in his anthology *Flame Wars: The Discourse of Cyberculture* to mean "speculative fiction that treats African-American themes and addresses African-American concerns in the context of 20th-century techno culture—and more generally, African-American signification that appropriates images of technology and a prosthetically enhanced future."[17] Dery also asks whether New World Africans, with the encumbrance of an occluded history, can "imagine possible futures," especially within a landscape dominated by the white hegemony in the socioeconomic arena and within the sci-fi genre. Buckell, Hopkinson, Lord, and a cadre of emerging black creative artists have been answering yes to that question. In fact, Kudwo Eshun advances the idea that science fiction operates according to a dialectic: "Science fiction was never concerned with the future, but rather with engineering feedback between its preferred future and its becoming present."[18] In an interview, Buckell echoes Eshun's recognition that sci-fi is concerned with shaping a relationship between present and future: "I felt that Caribbean people had a place in the future, and that if humanity were to populate the stars, that Caribbean people would immigrate in that great diaspora, and that they should have stories as well."[19] If, as the St. Lucian Nobel laureate Derek Walcott claims about the Caribbean, "The Sea is History," the title of a much-celebrated poem, perhaps the sky is a signifier of the future.[20]

In the essay "Afrofuturism, Science Fiction, and the History of the Future," Lisa Yaszek further defines the term "Afrofuturism" as "an extension of the historical recovery projects that black Atlantic intellectuals have engaged in for well over 200 years."[21] Yaszek also recognizes how blackness and dystopia are often linked: "It seems we are trapped in an historical moment when we can think about the future in terms of disaster—and that disaster is almost always associated with the racial other."[22] How do Caribbean sci-fi writers construct futuristic analogues of the region and its citizens, and how do they engage with the "disaster" to which Yaszek alludes? Buckell's writing provides an opportunity for trying to answer this question. His work is firmly installed in the broader sci-fi canon, and his Xenowealth series is widely acknowledged for its Caribbean-inspired setting and characters. Variously described as Caribbean cyberpunk, Caribbean steampunk, and Caribbean space opera, the series features protagonists—indeed, entire nations of people—of Caribbean descent who are exiled on a world light-years from Earth. By titling his series "Xenowealth," Buckell signals his intent to foreground the foreign, marginalized, and outsider status of the region, a status that has followed its citizen centuries into the future. But it is also a gesture toward a recovery of the region's history, because these Caribbean nationals have a counterpart community to the oppressive history of slavery and colonization associated with the paradoxically titled British Commonwealth.

Tobias Buckell and Xenowealth

Grenada-born Tobias Buckell is a prolific *New York Times* best-selling author of numerous novels and short stories. In a *Caribbean Beat* interview in 2016, Buckell responded to the question "What is it that makes Caribbean speculative fiction distinct?" by indicating that issues of empire and sovereignty are key.

> We've all had this experience of the Caribbean. It's like the Jamaican national motto—a sort of "out of many come one" situation. Each of us has come from a different island that has a different history, but when we get together and talk, there are all these commonalities. The island experience, concerns of dialect, concerns about deep history, about place in the world, diaspora, and empire, post-empire—those themes weave in and out of our work together. And yet the group is very Caribbean in that it's such a distinct mix of different people. That's what makes the Caribbean fascinating—it's not just one thing.
>
> My ideal reader is someone who enjoys *Star Wars* and lives in the Caribbean.[23]

The focus of Buckell's Xenowealth novels is a populace descended from Caribbean nationals who fled Earth many generations ago in search of refuge from an intergalactic hegemony. Language and cultural practices suggest that the ancestors of these people were from the Anglophone Caribbean;

FIGURE 1. Cover of *Sly Mongoose*, illustration by Todd Lockwood. From *Sly Mongoose* © 2008 by Tobias S. Buckell. Reprinted by permission of Tor / Forge Books, a division of Macmillan Publishing Group, LLC. All Rights Reserved.

additionally, their racial demographics mirror that of the Anglophone Caribbean: a majority are of African descent, with smaller but distinct populations of Asian and European descent. In *Crystal Rain*, the first novel of the series, as well as Buckell's first novel, the reader learns about the exodus of the original inhabitants of the Caribbean through a bedtime story: "A long time ago, all we old-father them had work on a cold world with no ocean or palm tree. It was far, far from this world. It was far, far from them own world, call Earth! They had to toil for Babylon. In return, Babylon oppress many people. And eventually them Babylon-oppress people ran away looking for a new world, a world far away from any other world so they could be left alone."[24] This description of the community's history is coded as the enslavement of Africans in the New World. In *Crystal Rain*, the people held in bondage are dislocated from their original habitat in the same way that Africans were during the transatlantic slave trade. The bedtime narrative alludes also to the enslavement of the Jews in Egypt, an event often constructed as an analogue of African slavery. Furthermore, the term "Babylon" is commonly used in the Caribbean to refer to historically discriminatory institu-

FIGURE 2. Cover of *Ragamuffin*, illustration by Todd Lockwood. From *Ragamuffin* © 2007 by Tobias S. Buckell. Reprinted by permission of Tor / Forge Books, a division of Macmillan Publishing Group, LLC. All Rights Reserved.

tions such as the police force. This longing for refuge and to be simply left alone takes the original inhabitants of the Caribbean on a multigalactic adventure over the course of many centuries. It is this recasting of the Caribbean's bid for sovereignty that occupies Buckell's attention throughout his first three novels, upon which this chapter is focused.

Crystal Rain

Crystal Rain features the typical characteristics of the steampunk genre, particularly Victorian era or industrial age technology such as steam engines, telegraphs, and hot air balloons. According to Eric Smith, "Buckell radically revises steampunk by relocating its geo-temporal coordinates from a first-world past to a third-world future, a structural inversion that transfigures the encumbering history casually shed by the former into the utopian destiny of the latter."[25] The novel is set on the planet of New Anegada, fondly referred to by the Caribbean-descended inhabitants as Nanagada. The planet's name is a nod to Anegada, the northernmost of the British Virgin Islands, also known as the "drowned land." While this epithet reflects the very low elevation of the real Anegada and acknowledges its susceptibility to flooding, it also aptly describes the precariousness of the fictional planet New Anegada and the vulnerability of its Caribbean inhabitants. The Nanagadans share the planet with the Azteca, a nation of people whom the novel describes as "religious fanatics."[26] Modeled on the Mexica, the Aztecas are obsessed with the Teotl, their bloodthirsty gods. These gods are in fact a race of technologically advanced aliens who can radically alter their appearance. The same bedtime story that introduces the history of the planet provides the history of the Teotl: "The evil Tetol come in from other worm's holes that had been all around for long time. You see, the Tetol is dangerous nasty things, who want to rule and own we all. But some other great beings, the Loa, weren't evil, but help and guide we against the Tetol."

The Nanagadans have their own internal religious and political unrest. There is a history of tension between the Loa—their gods—and their female prime minister, Dihana, who is consumed with the need to protect her country from an impending invasion by the Aztecas. They are kept out by a treacherous and almost impassable set of mountains—the Wicked Highs. Straddling the width of the peninsula occupied by the Nanagadans, they are patrolled by a stealthy grassroots military force known as the Mongoose Men. But unknown to the Nanagadans, the Aztecas have been digging a tunnel under the mountain, preparing to invade Nanagada at the behest of the Teotl. Essential to defeating the invaders is the novel's protagonist, John deBrun, a man who washed up on a beach almost thirty years ago with no memory of his past. Two other key characters are the antiheroes Pepper, a mysterious dreadlocked stranger who turns up in search of John, and Oaxyctl, a double agent planted by the Azteca.

The main action of the novel is set in motion when John and his family find an aviator and his airship tangled up in some mango trees in their backyard. The aviator has been shot but manages to give a solemn word of warning before he dies: "Azteca coming down the side of the mountain. Understand? Azteca. A lot of Azteca."[27] The remaining plot revolves around the attack of the Azteca on Nanagada and the convergence of the quests of the three main characters. John desperately wants to rescue his family and restore order to his community. Pepper wants to find John, with whom he has an extensive, multicentury history, and Oaxyctl simply wants to complete his mission and escape punishment from the gods.

The three end up together on a journey to the icy northern regions of Nanagada in search of the mysterious *Ma Wi Jung*, an interstellar spaceship bioengineered to interface with John's body and to respond only to him. The Nanagadans believe this powerful ship, hidden somewhere up north, is the lynchpin to victory against the Aztecas. With John on the edge of death, the trio locates the *Ma Wi Jung*, and this discovery precipitates a number of other insights. Additionally, John and Pepper become aware of Oaxyctl's deceit, and John begins to regain his memory. He discovers that he is many centuries old and that, like Pepper, he spent hundreds of years trapped in a pod, hurtling through space. This recuperation of memory, traumatic though it might be, is yoked to John's ability to pilot the *Ma Wi Jung* and to his eventual victory against the Aztecas, suggesting that an embrace of past trauma is a crucial step in overcoming current adversity.

He also discovers that he and Pepper were business partners. In fact, they are two of the "old fathers" referred to in the bedtime story that narrates the history of Nanagada. By the close of the novel, John and Pepper secure victory for Nanagada against the Aztecas and, further, embrace the responsibility of preventing the spread of colonizing and repressive forces: "If we don't get help, if we don't warn other worlds, the Teotl will wash over all the worlds like the tide."[28]

Buckell reconstitutes the Caribbean's history of enslavement and colonization in the future, and offers the reader an opportunity to imagine a past and a future driven by a persistent desire to be left alone. In this future history, Buckell challenges the wholesomeness of religion and interrogates religious dogma by exposing the uncritical embrace of questionable religious practices. For example, the novel graphically portrays the fanaticism of the Azteca, and John ends up witnessing the savage sacrifice of a Mongoose Man when they are both captured by the Azteca: "The priest straddled Alex, looked up into the sun, then plunged the knife into the supine man's ribs. Alex screamed. He screamed as the priest cut and snapped bone, and he didn't stop until the priest grunted with satisfaction. The tearing sound continued until a final whimper, and then the priest held Alex's dripping heart up toward the sun."[29] While the novel circumvents the usual black-white polarities in representing European–New World tensions, its portrayal of the Aztecas as savage strikes an uncomfortable chord, given the history of racist renderings of indigenous groups—indeed, of many black and brown colonized people.

In the essay "Tobias S. Buckell's Galactic Caribbean Future," Sharon DeGraw notes this aspect of the novel: "This revised colonialism clearly empowers the Azteca, but it also aligns them with the colonial oppressor and stresses the most negative attributes of their Aztec antecedents."[30] This problematic portrayal is primarily in service to Buckell's efforts to interrogate the role of religion in the formation and sustenance of hegemonies. These gruesome acts challenge the sanctity of religious practices, a challenge also facilitated by the portrayal of Oaxyctl's inner turmoil.[31] He is a double agent, gathering information about the Nanagadans for the Azteca while also spying on the Azteca for the Nanagadans. Oaxyctl desperately wants to be "noble" but is stymied by the gods' insistence on his doing their bidding and by his fear of the gods. Oaxyctl longs to simply complete the mission assigned to him by the Teotl and "return to Aztlan [home of the Azteca] and forget this foreign wilderness in the gods' good graces." Oaxyctl articulates the disastrous effect of religion on both the Nanagadans and the Azteca, attributing their conflict to their gods: "All our ancestors have been cast down from greatness. That is all we know for sure. All else is confused and muddied, because the Teotl, my people, your people, and the Loa that the Teotl have sworn to destroy are all in conflict."

Throughout the novel, John, Pepper, and Oaxyctl attempt to unburden themselves of their oppressive personal histories. Just as Oaxyctl is weighed down by the burden placed on him by the gods, John is burdened by his lack of memory, and Pepper must bear the memory of the centuries he spent isolated in an interstellar pod drifting through space while aching to get back home. All these personal quests for control of one's destiny replicate and engage with the angst and turmoil historically experienced by Caribbean people in the face of slavery, colonialism, and its postcolonial aftermath.

Crystal Rain further explores the quest for regional sovereignty by recasting historical arenas of oppression and bids for power. For example, the Aztecas attack and capture Nanagadans during the merriment of a carnival celebration. The unexpected arrival of the invaders and the suddenness of their attack bring to mind the hunting and capture of Africans during the Atlantic slave trade, an experience like the one that Olaudah Equiano described. Sharon DeGraw points out that "in one page, the reader is wrenched back to the colonial era, the slave trade, and the horrific slavery once practiced in the Caribbean."[32]

Other bids for sovereignty that the novel reconstitutes are the postslavery efforts of regional leaders such as Marcus Garvey and organizations like the Universal Negro Improvement Association (UNIA) to foster black economic independence. The UNIA founded the Black Star Line, intended to facilitate trade and movement across the African diaspora. Both John and Pepper, who are cyborgs, founded the Black Starliner Corporation and are longtime partners in the business.[33] Hundreds of years ago, this fleet transported Caribbean-descended populations to the safety of new planets in the face of alien oppression. By naming the corporation after Garvey's company, Buckell splices together the historical desire of Caribbean people for self-determination with a similar, futuristic effort by the Nanagadans to obtain independence. The novel is an effort to engineer a conversation between the past and future, one in which painful aspects of the Caribbean's history are revisited and rewritten.

Ragamuffin

The title of *Ragamuffin*, the second in the Xenowealth series, refers to a motley set of space bandits known as Ragamuffin, or Raga, who are described as "pirates and smugglers, plying the lonely spaceways around a dead wormhole."[34] Like its predecessor, *Ragamuffin* focuses on the descendants of Caribbean nationals. It opens in a world ruled by an alien race known as the Benevolent Satrapy, which oversees an empire of forty-eight worlds accessible via a series of wormholes. Humans are held in quasi bondage, forced to endure control by the Satraps, who closely regulate humans' use of technology and limit their interstellar movement. In some parts of the galaxy, another alien race, the Gahe, keep humans as pets. The planets Chimson and New Anegada have become the refugees' new homes. But when Chimson successfully revolted and won its freedom from Satrap control, the wormhole that gave its inhabitants access to the rest of the galaxy was shut down, and they became disconnected from other humans. For years, the Benevolent Satrapy has tolerated them, but no longer. The plot of *Ragamuffin* centers on Nashara. She is from the line of Jamal, the man who led the Caribbean exiles to freedom centuries earlier. Nashara, a fugitive, is desperate to get home to Chimson. She is also a cyborg; her womb was removed and replaced with an atomic device.

The Satrapic Empire is clearly an allusion to the European colonial system. Like European colonizers, the Satraps exert control over the mobility and economic activities of their subjects. Buckell complicates this representation by coding the Satrapy as a symbolic representation of the Unites States: the Satraps preside over forty-eight worlds, analogous to the forty-eight states in the contiguous United States. Buckell makes other connections with the history of the New World. References to the Black Starliner Corporation again appear. We discover that the Ragamuffin ships were part of the original fleet that transported Caribbean refugees to safety, gesturing toward the black diaspora and the historical role of the Black Starliner Corporation in enabling both the exodus and the underground economy of Caribbean people.

Furthermore, each Ragamuffin ship has an Afrocentric name: *Queen Mohmbasa*, *Cudjo*, *Duppy Conqueror*. One is called the *Cornell West*. These names further connote the ships' function as incubators and carriers of a lost connection with a homeland, and of a Caribbean and African diasporic cultural legacy. Additionally, several of the Ragamuffin crew sport dreadlocks; their speech uses Caribbean syntax and Creole vocabulary; and they refer to elements of Caribbean folklore such as Anancy the spider. When there is crisis and the Raga captains have to meet, they call a "grounation," a term common in Rastafarian parlance to refer to the day that commemorates Emperor Haile Selassie's visit to Jamaica in 1966.[35] Sharon DeGraw elucidates the implications of this continuity: "Buckell's fictional reworking transforms slaves, involuntarily transported, into dynamic and autonomous explorers, settlers, and traders. Those once kept illiterate now have the technology to travel through worm holes and terraform planets."[36]

Aside from anchoring elements of the novel in Caribbean history and culture, Buckell engages with a number of contemporary political and economic debates facing the region, such as issues around mobility and access to resources. The movement of these Caribbean descendants is circumscribed by the Satraps, who engage in extensive surveillance. The Ragamuffin ships, sometimes referred to as higgler ships, function as analogues of modern-day

Caribbean higglers (informal commercial traders); both circumvent bureaucratic barriers to the global economies from which they have traditionally been cut off. The description of the ships also alludes to the illicit drug trade: "Ragamuffin ships smuggled anything black market, as well as a shitload of illegal tech. Nothing new there."[37]

The Hongguo is the human military arm of the Satraps. It is charged with monitoring and controlling piracy, technological development, and illegal trade among the humans. The Hongguo functions much like an amalgamation of Homeland Security, the militarized police, and the Border Patrol. Its agents can restrict mobility as punishment because they have oversight of visa distribution: "Usually the Hongguo put up a stink just outside legal lane areas, boarded a ship, and combed it thoroughly. Punishment involved heavy fines, loss of visa privileges to a given system."[38]

Nashara, like many Caribbean nationals living in a metropole today, is isolated and stranded, unable to get home to Chimson. The trajectory of the novel follows her state of exile and her longing to return to her planet. Nashara suffers from the familiar postcolonial malady of being forcefully shut off from home: "There was no Earth, no Chimson, and no New Anegada for her to go to. Just humanity scuttling around underfoot of their alien superiors. She had no home. Any future would involve running."[39] DeGraw explains that this construction of Nashara valorizes her: "While enduring much physical and mental suffering, Nashara does so willingly and comes across as a hero rather than a victim. In this way, Buckell can simultaneously allude to both the unequal suffering and heroic resistance of Afro-Caribbeans in the historical context of slavery, and people of color in western colonialism more broadly."[40] In short, Nashara's personal bid for independence symbolizes the ongoing efforts of the region to exercise sovereignty.

Sly Mongoose

Sly Mongoose, Buckell's third novel, is set on the planet Chilo, where the atmosphere is so deadly to human life that people have to live in floating cities thousands of feet above the surface of the planet. With temperatures in excess of 800 degrees, "sulphuric rain," and "hurricanelike winds," Chilo's deadly atmosphere is "a monstrous perpetual storm."[41] (The protagonist is fourteen-year-old Timas, whose economic circumstances force him to do the dangerous yet prestigious job of *xocoyotzin* (a Nahuatl word meaning "honored young one"), which involves maintaining the equipment that mines valuable ore on Chilo's dangerous surface. To do this, he must wear a cumbersome protective groundsuit that weighs over fifty pounds and is too small to fit most adults. The result is that aside from working under treacherous circumstances, he must constantly guard against putting on weight. If he is unable to fit into his groundsuit, he risks losing his job as a *xocoyotzin* and all the benefits the job provides for him and his family. As a result, Timas has become bulimic, constantly fretting about putting on weight and becoming unable to fit into his suit.

Timas is Azteca, and it was his ancestors who attacked New Anegada in *Crystal Rain*. The novel explains how his people wound up on Chilo: "When the Azteca of New Anegada left aboard ships bound for other planets, trying to escape their history there, had they ever imagined ending up on a world like this?"[42] Timas and other Azteca live in the floating city of Yatapek, a site characterized as underdeveloped, most of its population socially and economically marginalized. For example, Timas is a *xocoyotzin* because only boys of his size can fit in the protective suits; Yatapek cannot afford larger suits to fit adult men. The portholes of the elevators that lower Timas and other *xocoyotzin* thousands of feet to Chilo's surface have been damaged, and Yatapek is unable to replace them. The radios that the *xocoyotzin* use to communicate with one another and that the city uses to communicate with other cities and spacecraft have fallen into disrepair, and Yatapek does not have the resources to fix them. As a result, the city has only a few operational radios. Young men like Timas and his friend Cen, who dies in an unfortunate accident, are consistently overwhelmed with anxiety about keeping their jobs, since they are the main breadwinners for their families, which hover on the edge of poverty.

The other civilization central to the novel is the Aeolians. They too live in floating cities far above Chilo's surface, but they have much greater wealth than the Aztecans. The Aeolians are coded as a developed nation, and their name alludes to the mythical floating island of Aeolia, which Odysseus encounters on his journey in the *Odyssey*. The Aeolians in Buckell's novel have access to advanced technology and consequently are able to mine the natural resources they need from asteroids.[43] This control of vital resources is also a feature of the mythical floating island of Aeolia, home to Aeolus, the keeper of winds, who is able to control when and where powerful winds are unleashed.[44] Because the Aeolians in Buckell's novel are similarly powerful, they do not need to put their children in danger by sending them to the lethal surface of Chilo. Aside from living much more comfortably than the Aztecans, the Aeolians are a potential source of assistance in a crisis, functioning much like the World Bank or the International Monetary Fund in those organizations' relationships with developing countries today. Katrina, an Aeolian girl visiting Yatapek, is Timas's age. She is doing national service as part of a diplomatic mission, and Timas ends up being assigned to host her. Both Timas and Katrina provide child labor for their countries, but Katrina under circumstances much more comfortable than the dangerous ones Timas must endure. These differences between Timas and Katerina, between those on Yatapek and those in the Aeolian cities, clearly refer to the contemporary social and economic divide between developing and developed countries.

The main action of the novel is set in motion when Pepper comes crashing through Yatapek's dome after deorbiting from a spaceship. Pepper is intent on warning the city about the Swarm, an approaching invasion of zombies. The plot of the novel centers on this impending invasion, and Pepper ends up joining forces with Timas and Katrina to try and prevent it. By the end of the novel, we discover that the zombie attack is an act of bioterrorism, and after a bloody battle between humans and the Swarm, the humans emerge victorious.

The disparities within Yatapek society and between those on Yatapek and those in the Aeolian cities are stark, represented in great part through Timas's character and his ambivalence about working as a *xocoyotzin*. He is adored, even venerated, by his family, which depends tremendously on his status as a *xocoyotzin* for their own status, comfort, and survival. Because of Timas's job, the family is able to live in the upper levels of Yatapek. The lower and middle layers resemble present-day tenements. The houses are described as "jammed together" in "tight alleyways, dirty and filled with litter," and the neighborhood smells like "body odor and frying oil."[45] These lower levels replicate many of the worst conditions of contemporary urban slums in the developing world. In contrast, Timas lives in a well-constructed house with a courtyard, and his family has servants. The fragility of Timas's position is made starkly clear when his coworker Cen is killed on the surface of Chilo. Shortly after his death, Cen's entire family is expelled from their comfortable dwelling in the upper layers and sent to the less desirable lower layers. As they make their departure, in the middle of the night, Timas watches from his bedroom window: "Cen's older brother, Luc, pulled a large wooden cart along the road. Bundles of clothing, furniture, and chests hastily stacked on it swayed about, threatening to fall out . . . No longer the family of xocoyotzin, they moved now to the lower levels, looking for jobs where the city crowded on top of itself, where little light reached the buildings, and the alleys smelled of humanity, industry, and badly recycled air."

Timas's circumstances further reflect the complexities of contemporary culture because he must make himself bulimic in order to do his work as a *xocoyotzin*. Because of the family's dependence on Timas, he makes himself vomit after meals as a means of controlling his weight. This behavior is sanctioned by his family, and on one occasion his mother asks whether he has vomited up enough of his meal. Timas's illness is such an integrated aspect of his life that he has a "small polished wooden dowel" in a "ceremonial cup" sitting beside his sink.[46] Timas is also anorexic, and as he prepares for his trips to the surface, he starves himself by eating nothing but vegetables to ensure he can fit into the groundsuit. Timas's eating disorders embody in many ways the tensions in the modern West between surplus that must be dispelled and shortage.

Sly Mongoose explores another feature of the modern West—democratic rule. The novel plays with the West's ideological embrace of this system of government by literalizing its portrayal. Avatars like Katrina act in concert with their entire society, and she relies heavily on consensus in the decision-making process. As a result, she turns presumptions about the effectiveness of democratic governance on their head. Katrina explains that Aeolians are "live voting" on what she should say as she interacts with the officials on Yatapek.[47] This extreme construction of democracy comes across as a caricature of modern Western democratic practices and could also allude to the practice of direct democracy in ancient Athens, given the historical significance of the planet's name in Greek myth. This hyper-democracy is facilitated by the cyborg nature of many Aeolians. For example, one of Katrina's eyes is mechanized so that she can transmit all she sees back to the rest of Aeolian society. In earlier times, when Aeolian technology was not as advanced, emissaries would sometimes take extended amounts of time to respond to questions while awaiting communal approval of their intended responses. The "awkward pauses and blank looks" they sometimes displayed earned Aeolians the nickname "zombies." This moniker gestures toward the Swarm zombies attacking Chilo, perhaps implying that the collective behavior of Western societies is not unlike the thoughtless and robotic behavior of the Swarm.

That the Aeolians represent a developed-world culture is further supported by their tourism to Yatapek. Like much of the developing world today, Yatapek serves as a place where the wealthy can fulfill touristic desires. Again, the relationship models many of the dynamics between well-off tourists and destinations in poor countries, and comments on the constrained mobility of black and brown people across the planet: "[The Aeolians] liked to fly out to Yatapek to enjoy the large and open upper layer for vacations. No wide-open spaces in their packed cities. Handmade crafts from the lower level markets also attracted them. For the Aeolians the price of a flight here cost little, even though most on Yatapek could not afford to leave."[48]

At the end of *Sly Mongoose*, the Swarm is halted by the collaborative efforts of the Aeolians, the Ragamuffins, and the population of Yatapek. The novel constructs a future in which race has transcended the complexity surrounding it in the contemporary, postcolonial world. The Aeolians are mostly black or pale, and only a few are brown like Katrina. This upending of the dominant color hierarchies of the past several centuries forces the reader to contemplate discrimination and racial marginalization through characters who are not freighted with current anxieties surrounding black and white racial polarities. According to Sharon DeGraw, "A unique feature of Buckell's science fictional retelling of slavery is that it centers on black subjectivity and elides any Anglo participation. Buckell is not interested in the complex black/white relationships of slavery which fascinate so many other writers, or Anglo colonialism. Although this largely relieves the Anglos of responsibility for (terrestrial) colonialism and slavery, . . . the primary intent is to increase the representation of people of color, despite Buckell's familial connections to Anglos."[49]

All of the settings in the novels are established as locations that have in great part transcended the usual pitfalls of race and the marginalization of people of color. The conflict at the core of each novel is not a racial replication of the black-white antagonisms central to postcolonial politics. DeGraw suggests that Buckell's writing "offers an alternate, positive model of race consciousness which reflects the greater inclusion of post-colonial writers in science fiction."[50]

Additionally, all three novels engineer a conversation between the future and the past, suggesting that the survival of the Caribbean rests with the capacity for resistance inherent in regional cooperation and the development and deployment of Caribbean technological expertise. For example, the Mongoose Men and the Ragamuffins are Caribbean militia groups that grew out of the battle of Caribbean-descended people for freedom from the oppression of alien forces vying to control them. These militia groups and the men and women associated with them, such as John deBrun, Nashara, and Pepper, end up saving the day in each of the novels, functioning in many respects as black superheroes. The names that Buckell gives these groups signify marginalization and, in many ways, blackness. "Ragamuffin" in its general sense refers to a street urchin. This term has found favor in Afro-Caribbean culture not only as a reference to disenfranchised youth but also as an evocation of dancehall music. Dancehall often features songs with themes about black marginalization and oppression, and the term appears in dancehall songs such as "Ragamuffin Soldier" by Daddy Freddy.

The animal known as a mongoose holds a similarly marginalized position in the region and is generally seen as a predatory pest. In fact, the mongoose and the region's black population in some ways share a parallel history of being introduced to support the colonial economic machinery, but then becoming disruptive and demanding of additional resources. Introduced into the region in the nineteenth century to help control rats, mongooses eventually became a nuisance themselves. Lacking natural enemies, they proliferated so much that they turned to other food sources such as poultry. The figure of the sly mongoose appears in works of Caribbean oral literature such as the Anancy stories, as well as in songs, where it is generally characterized as a crafty thief. In many song versions, including one recorded by Lord Invader, a mongoose manages to sneak into a kitchen and steal a fowl. The third novel of the series uses the name, but in all the Xenowealth novels, subaltern populations find ways to sabotage the system and infiltrate it for their own interests—just as the mongoose has done in the Caribbean. Mongooses and ragamuffins are bonded by the much-maligned reputation they share. That important organizations in the novels bearing these names are key to overcoming an enormous threat in each novel recommends the value of incorporating the marginalized into a pan-Caribbean body politic in order to successfully navigate the future.

Tobias Buckell graciously agreed to an interview with me (see the appendix to this volume), and his comments provide thought-provoking context for critically engaging with his work. The deep yearning for home experienced by many of his characters and sustained as a key element of the plot of each novel in the trilogy finds resonance with Buckell's own life. Buckell notes the liminality of his subject position as a somewhat displaced Caribbean national, like his main characters in the three novels. He discusses the liminal nature of the life he had when he lived in the Caribbean, moving between islands and sometimes living on a boat. He describes himself as an "in-between sort of person" who does not see home as a single geographic location, but as "the amalgamation of my memories and relationships from both Grenada and the Virgin Islands." His characters experience home and acknowledge their Caribbean ancestry similarly, perhaps as something more indistinct than a personal memory, since they are in many cases descendants of the original inhabitants of the Caribbean and have come to identify with the region only through the narratives passed down to them by their communities.

He further establishes his personal sense of in-betweenness, explaining that one parent was British and the other an "islander." In reference to his status as an immigrant, Buckell asks: "Am I someone who will be rooted, family oriented, or am I a wanderer, doomed to pull up and move on soon? Then as an immigrant to the U.S., I become an outsider who lives there while then being an outsider to the Caribbean." It is this same sense of perpetual itinerancy and indeterminate citizenship that his characters experience, ever wondering when they will be able to enjoy the stability of Caribbean nationhood.

Buckell passionately agrees with Nalo Hopkinson's critique that sci-fi "speaks so much about the experience of being alienated, but contains so little written by alienated people themselves."[51] He contends that mainstream sci-fi often constructs rebellion narratives in which success is due to the determination of a few characters. According to Buckell, this trope "ignores the brutality of slavery and colonization in those stories and how hard and infrequent successful revolts were." Buckell further explains that he sees Caribbean sci-fi as a unique literary expression that does not easily fit in what one might consider the most suitable literary genre—Afrofuturism: "I do think there are some key differences between the African American experience and the Caribbean experience that, despite tremendous places of overlap, don't fit together, and this affects the fiction." Buckell suggests that having political sovereignty and access to national histories influences the differences he sees in Caribbean sci-fi.

When asked about the Caribbean as inspiration, he explained that its ever-present influence on his work is sometimes obscure. It can be seen in a story he wrote about a robot working on a spaceship: "In some ways, the setting is classic big-idea space opera SF. But the character, the idea for the story, the resonance in it, all came from my reading about work-resistance strategies of pre-independent Caribbean islands. It's one of the most Caribbean things I've written, as far as its inception. Yet it won't seem that way to most." In fact, he notes that the most memorable response to his work from a Caribbean reader was that it was not "exotic" enough, providing too many perfectly replicated features common to life in the Caribbean. The Caribbean reader noted, "If they wanted to go outside to the bush, they'd step out into their backyard, and if they wanted to read about the food in their kitchen, they'd just get up and go eat it. They wanted to go somewhere truly alien!" For Buckell, this was validation that he had "nailed the flavor" of the region. He was so excited about this review that he printed it and put it up on his wall.

Fredric Jameson suggests that the purpose of science fiction is "not to give us 'images' of the future . . . but rather to defamiliarize and restructure our experience with our own *present*, and to do so in specific ways distinct from all other forms of defamiliarization."[52] This kind of future history is what Buckell constructs in his first three novels. He manages to shape a futuristic Caribbean space that acknowledges the trauma of the region's history on an intergalactic stage by reconstituting historical efforts to gain independence from both slavery and a global economic system that limits access and opportunities. Buckell uses the fantastic in the form of science fiction to comment on slavery, colonialism, and race relations while simultaneously emphasizing a contemporary postcolonial reality. His novels shape a space in which the Caribbean fantastic fosters a reimagining of the colonial experience and its aftermath as one in which those who claim Caribbean heritage are invested in the region's sovereignty and committed to a path of self-determination. Though science fiction achieves its fantastical nature via an uncanny encounter with familiar technology functioning in unfamiliar ways, it does the same work as more traditional conceptions of the fantastic such as hauntings and sorcery. Furthermore, Buckell's writing supports the theoretical arguments made by John Rieder and Isiah Lavender that are mentioned earlier in this chapter. It engages with matters of colonialism, and although race is rarely mentioned, it is frequently invoked and coded through cultural markers such as language, hair, and cuisine. Additionally, Buckell's trilogy suggests that access to technology will be a key component of the Caribbean's ability to exercise sovereignty in the future.

Derek Walcott asserts, "In the Caribbean history is irrelevant, not because it is not being created, or because it was sordid; but because it has never mattered. What has mattered is the loss of history, the amnesia of the races, what has become necessary is imagination, imagination as necessity, as invention."[53] It is this act of imagining, called for by Walcott in 1973, before Buckell was born, to which Buckell responds, writing out of necessity, writing as an act of resistance. As Buckell argues, many narratives by white sci-fi writers treat as irrelevant "the brutality of slavery (and colonization in those stories) and how hard and infrequent successful revolts were." This paucity of counternarratives propels his writing, and he seeks to offer his reader both an alternative history and a desired future in which the region in victorious in claiming its sovereignty each time it is challenged.

Aside from adhering to the idea of "imagination as necessity, as invention," to which he refers in the interview, Buckell helps avoid "the danger of a single story," the title of Chimamanda Ngozi Adichie's popular TED talk, in which she asserts the importance of attending to a variety of voices in the narration of history.[54] In the essay "Black to the Future," featured in the collection *Dark Matter*, Walter Mosley writes: "The power of science fiction is that it can tear down the walls and windows, the artifice and laws by changing the logic, empowering the disenfranchised, or simply by asking, What if?"[55] What if the African diaspora can reimagine Olaudah Equiano's capture and forced exile on a vessel unknown to him, controlled by strange-looking beings, and envision instead a world full of people who look like him manning their own ships, zooming trough wormholes from one world to the next, and successfully combatting alien strangers who want to control their lives, even hold them as pets? What if, Buckell's trilogy asks, the Caribbean could revisit the moment of colonization and shed the weight of imperialist rule? What if?

CONCLUSION

Seeing Strange Things

Fantastical Visual Portrayals of the Caribbean

> Española is a marvel; the mountains and hills, and plains, and fields, and the soil, so beautiful and rich for planting and sowing.... There could be no believing, without seeing, such harbors as are here, as well as the many and great rivers, and excellent waters, most of which contain gold.
>
> CHRISTOPHER COLUMBUS TO
> LUIS DE SANTANGEL, FEBRUARY 15, 1493

Caribbean visual artists have a deeply evident attachment to a fantastical imaginary of the region. Many of the artists who emerged in the first half of the twentieth century were intimately associated with Afro-Caribbean spiritual practices, which profoundly inflected their work. These include Cuba's Wifredo Lam, Trinidad's LeRoy Clarke, Haiti's Hector Hyppolite, and Jamaica's Mallica "Kapo" Reynolds. The work of several contemporary Caribbean artists such as Brian Wong Won (Trinidad), Marcel Pinas (Suriname), and Jose Bedia (Cuba) sustains this engagement with the metaphysical in varied and compelling ways. For example, Wong Won, who is known for his colorful renderings of carnival scenes, creates images that evoke the transformative magic associated with the carnival space, such as his whimsical series of "dancing houses," which suggests the fantastical capacity of carnival.[1] Additionally, his picturesque characters are garbed in costumes that explicitly refer to spirits and ghouls, and they demonstrate the liminality and hybridity of the carnival space, since they are costumed to look like both man and beast, both human and spirit. In addition to coding hybridity, the

FIGURE 3. Brian Wong Won, *Carnival Joy*.
A depiction of carnival festivities in Trinidad.

costuming in the scenes as well as the chaos of color and obscured view of the setting suggest the fluid nature of the carnival space.

For other artists, the fantastic informs their work in a way that results in a much less cheerful aesthetic. One of the best-known contemporary Caribbean artists whose work is significantly informed by the fantastic is the Haitian-born Miami-based artist Edouard Duval-Carrié. My interest in the Caribbean visual arts has been particularly inspired by his work, which deeply provoked and unsettled me from the instant I came across it many years ago in the Lowe Art Museum as a graduate student at the University of Miami. Known for his colorful portrayals of the region, his fervent engagement with some of the most troubling historical and contemporary problems facing Haiti and the Caribbean, and his lavish deployment of the fantastic, Duval-Carrié is a celebrated artist who commands national and global attention. His expansive corpus of work has been the subject of numerous critical studies. In *Continental Shifts: The Art of Edouard Duval-Carrié*, Edward Sullivan explains that "much of his art concerns issues of spirituality, violence in contemporary society, the ravages of war, exile and displacement, all of which are highly poignant for today's strife-torn societies world-wide."[2] Sullivan notes also that "in any discussion of the art of Edouard Duval-Carrié, we are obliged to turn our attention to his deep interest in the religious-based imagery of Haitian religion."

The piece I most remember from that museum visit was indeed heavily invested in Haitian spirituality. It was an enormous, stunning painting of a beautiful black woman with a baby swaddled to her waist as she descends, feet bare, from a U.S. Coast Guard cutter, escorted by armed guardsmen. The bejeweled woman is magnificently garbed in a ruffled pink dress, and heart-shaped images (as well as a dagger) float in the air around her head, drawing attention to the shadow of a halo. She appears unperturbed by the military presence as she grooms her hair. In fact, her calm and confident demeanor suggests that perhaps the men are her bodyguards. The woman is the Vodun loa Erzulie, and the piece is titled *Ezili Intercepted*. In one of her aspects, Erzulie is a love goddess much like Venus or Aphrodite, affiliated with the sea, but she is also known as a defender of children and women and an exacter of revenge. For me, the appeal of the painting lay in its engagement with the ubiquitous photos in South Florida newspapers of the Coast Guard corralling bewildered Haitians who had been intercepted at sea en route to Miami. April Shemak suggests that Erzulie "is poised in the limbo gateway on the gang plank of the Coast Guard ship" and that "she unites the spiritual world with the living."[3] This painting offers a representative example of how Duval-Carrié's work, which is heavily imbued with an aesthetic of the fantastic, comments on the often-embattled position of Haiti in relation to forces in the region and beyond. His paintings upend circulating discourses about the country's presumed fragility and subjection to tragedy, offering instead counternarratives such as *Ezili Intercepted* that reject this subaltern identity and expose the role of hegemonic forces in the nation's suffering.[4]

One of Duval-Carrié's most recently completed series is a set of ink-on-paper drawings based on the Cuban writer Alejo Carpentier's masterpiece *The Kingdom of This World*, which has been an ongoing source of inspiration for him. He read the novel as a teenager and was amazed that its fantastical portrayal of Haitian history coincided with his perspective on his home.[5] He was so inspired by the book that one of his earliest paintings featured Macandal (aka Makandal or Mackandal), a historical figure and key character in the novel, with insect wings. Duval-Carrié noted that "the figure of Macandal in Carpentier's recounting is about what is most fantastic in Haitian lore, things such as loup-garous [werewolves], soucouyants [malignant witches], changelings, and zombies."[6] Duval-Carrié's fascination with the Caribbean fantastic is clearly shown in his work, and that the plot of *The Kingdom of This World* would inspire a series of his drawings is no surprise.

Hailed as an early example of literary magical realism, *The Kingdom of This World* is set in the decades before and after the Haitian Revolution and unfolds during the life of a slave named Ti Noel. His fellow slave Macandal loses his hand in a cane mill, and in the aftermath, he absconds from the plantation to engage in a self-designed study of the magical properties of local plants. Macandal eventually acquires the ability to transform into various animals, a skill he later teaches to Ti Noel. Using this mystical knowledge, Macandal launches a revolt in the surrounding area through a series of poisonings. Macandal is eventually caught and burnt at the stake.

Ti Noel's owner flees to Cuba, where he loses the slave in a card game. Ti Noel eventually buys his freedom and returns to Haiti. The country, though under the reign of the black King Henri Christophe, continues to suffer. By the end of the novel, the king has committed suicide, and the country's new mulatto powerbrokers turn out to be just as barbaric as the French slaveholders. Ti Noel decides to use his shape-shifting skills to change into various animals, providing himself with new perspectives from which to observe the ever-unfolding turbulence around him.

Duval-Carrié's series of drawings offers a visual interpretation of Carpentier's work that foregrounds the magical-realist elements of the novel. In contrast to the vivid colors often associated with Duval-Carrié's art, this series is delicately laid out in blue ink on white paper. One piece in the series, *La Main Broyé* ("The Ground Hand"), depicts Macandal's hand being lost to the cane crusher. This scene represents the violence done to black and brown people in the New World and perhaps speaks to how the labors of people of color to overcome the historical disadvantages of colonialism and slavery remain hobbled by a missing limb. *Mastiffs Cubain* ("Cuban Mastiffs") features the dogs that Ti Noel sees being loaded onto a ship heading for Haiti, where they are intended to "eat niggers."[7] This drawing includes close-up perspectives of the dogs, which are portrayed as monstrous and even demonic, our attention drawn to their sharp teeth and wild gazes.

FIGURE 4. Edouard Duval-Carrié, *La Grotte des poisons*, ink on paper, 14" × 20", 2017. From a series of works illustrating Alejo Carpentier's novel *The Kingdom of This World*. On display in the artist's studio, Little Haiti, Miami, Florida. Photograph by the author.

Another of these images, *La Grotte des poisons* ("The Cave of Poisons") features Macandal, one hand missing, stirring a large pot over an open flame. Scattered around the cave are smaller pots bubbling over a fire, bottles, and what appears to be tree branches. In the background are stalactites positioned along the oval frame of the scene, like teeth growing from the yawning mouth of the cave. Filling the background are stalagmites protruding up from the floor of the cave. These resemble decapitated trees and allude to Duval-Carrié's signature image of exposed tree roots. The mutilated trees are surely in conversation with Macandal's severed hand, lost to the savage violence of slavery, and evoke an eerie spiritual presence.

La Grotte des poisons, like the other drawings in the series, is embedded in an oval and framed by delicately drawn floral patterns that seem to encode the propriety and order that was often projected as foundational to European social structure, especially in contrast to the presumed savagery of Africa. But Duval-Carrié uses this delicate imagery in contrast with the mutilated horror of slavery. I selected this image for the cover because it reflects the essence of what *Working Juju* asserts, namely, that the deployment of the fantastic from within the region often operates as a counternarrative to artifacts from outside the region, such as the texts written by Froude, Edwards, Long, Lewis, and Earle, discussed in chapter 1. Unlike the deployment of the fantastic in the hands of European writers who pathologized the region and masked the ravaging effects of the colonial project and its aftermath, the fantastic is often deployed from within the region to critique the legacy of imperialism and the ensuing imbricated discourses of suffering and abuse in their many forms. In *La Grotte des poisons*, Macandal is engaged in the literal act of working juju as he mixes his poisonous brew, and it reflects how people affiliated with the region, such as Tobias Buckell in his futuristic novels about the Caribbean, invoke the fantastic in different acts of juju.

Another contemporary Caribbean artist who deploys the fantastic in his work is Asser Saint-Val. Also born in Haiti, Saint-Val, like Duval-Carrié, is now based in South Florida, and his work is somewhere on the outer edge of the fantastic, featuring amorphous images that amalgamate human, animal, plant, and machine characteristics. Elements of these figures usually resemble familiar items like feathers, wheels, human limbs, and internal body parts like the brain or blood vessels, and some have a textured surface that resembles an enhanced, microscopic view of the skin. Saint-Val's creatures are generally suspended above the ground and positioned so that the horizon is in view. They also have some kind of inorganic mechanized component such as propellers. The images that result are uncanny hybrid creatures that are both startling and vaguely familiar. Almost all the images feature the limb of a white person, mostly a hand, which is positioned on the boundary of the painting so that the owner of the limb is offstage, so to speak, and the rest of the person's body is not visible to the viewer. The hand is usually signaling in same manner—pointing or beckoning—toward Saint-Val's creation. His paintings mostly feature bright colors, and he incorporates "a blend of traditional art mediums and a wide range of unconventional, organic materials—coffee, chocolate, ginger, tea and chocolate."[8]

Saint-Val kindly granted me an opportunity to meet with him to discuss his work. He explained that the unusual images he creates are inspired by an obsession he has had for years with the pigment melanin.[9] His interest developed after he moved from Haiti to the United States as a teenager and experienced the antagonistic responses that his blackness sometimes provoked. This was unfamiliar to him and created a deep longing to understand what it was about being black that propelled all the assumptions people made about who he was. He particularly notes his confusion about the fears people exhibited toward him because of his race. Overwhelmed by the racism he faced and deeply curious about its cause, he set out to accomplish what amounts to the dissection of racism in order to understand the basis for its existence. He pursued this idea by first comprehending the biological basis of darkly pigmented skin, and he has since been grappling with this pigment, melanin, which is responsible for the discrimination he has experienced, as a path to the exploration of race and racism.

Saint-Val's work features exceptionally unusual interpretations of this pigment, portraying it as whimsical creatures that defy easy definition. His website articulates his unusual and extreme fascination with melanin: "The molecular structure of the compound and the way it operates in the human body are suggestive sources of poetic possibility at the macro level, and are most powerfully linked in his [Saint-Val's] thought and representational practice to profound ideas about the human relationship to the matter and mechanics of the cosmos."[10] Furthermore, his website describes his work as "a surreal fantasia on such loosely linked themes as under-recognized African American inventors, the politics of sexual desire, and the complex aesthetics, narratives and metaphors that attach to the organic compounds neuromelanin."

Saint-Val's images are always set against the horizon, and many are airborne, hovering above the ground, or in motion on the ground, implied by the outstretched human legs that are a hallmark of many of his creations. The vantage point from which we see the image set against the horizon, as well as its implied movement (on the surface of the earth or in the air), suggests the transnational nature of the impact of melanin. Additionally, the amalgamation of human, plant, animal, and machinery parts into these images speaks to how concerns about physical and cultural hybridity inform his work. His images defy taxonomy, in contradistinction to how melanin has been the basis for quite expansive categorization pursuits. These categorizations have resulted in the emergence of terminology such as mulatto, quadroon, *dougla*, and mestizo as attempts to quantify and circumscribe the presence of melanin, as well as other genetic characteristics, in human beings.

His images also grapple with movement and mobility, signaled not only by their portrayals of motion but also by the way devices that accommodate movement are featured, such as wheels and propellers. There are few distinct suggestions of human identity aside from the limbs projecting from the amorphous shapes. These arms or legs perhaps refer to the experience of constraint and even entrapment often associated with the experience of blackness. Furthermore, the disembodied and somewhat indistinct hands or feet of a white person appear in most of his work and seem to be stand-ins for the white hegemony that continues to hold power over the global marketplace. The mechanized elements of each scene are reminiscent of the Victorian and industrial era mechanizations seen in steampunk, implying both physical movement and technological progress. Furthermore, Saint-Val's obsession with a pigment that is invisible to the human eye perhaps speaks to his concerns about black invisibility.

In our discussion, Saint-Val provided some useful insight into his work. He explained that his process for creating each piece is "chaotic" and does not involve deliberate thought, aside from research to identify the invention he will include. He further clarified that the items which I read as evocations of steampunk were in fact inventions for which the patent is held by a black person. He believes that knowledge about these accomplishments has been suppressed, and he wants his art to recognize and honor the work of black inventors. He also explained the unusual naming convention for his pieces. They bear odd, lumbering titles such as *Vigh-Teichmann. I., 1980. "Comparison of the Pineal Complex and Cerebrospinal Fluid . . ." Fuesch. Leipzig, 94, 623–640*. Another is titled *Swaab, D. F. and Visser, M. (1977) A function for alpha-MSH in fetal development and the presence of an alpha-MSH-like compound in nervous tissue. Frontiers in Hormone Research, 4, 170178 2006*. These names are citations for published articles relating to melanin. He uses the titles to further publicize information about this pigment. Saint-Val also discussed his earlier work, which featured nude women with skin in shades of red. He explained that these were his initial efforts to engage in a visual conversation about melanin, and certainly these images disrupt typical expectations about how skin color should be portrayed.

There are few easily recognizable connections among the components of each of Saint-Val's paintings, and the work seems to meet the definition of surrealism: "the principles, ideals, or practice of producing fantastic or incongruous imagery or effects in art, literature, film, or theater by means of unnatural or irrational juxtapositions and combinations."[11] Furthermore, André Breton, credited as the founder of surrealism, defines it as a complete circumvention of logical thought and an unmediated connection to the self.[12] Surprisingly, Saint-Val does not see himself as a surrealist; he simply naturally sees everything as connected. It is the contrast between the representation of the Caribbean in the work of artists such as Wong Won, Duval-Carrié, and Saint-Val, and the region's representation in a work like *Obi; or, The History of Three-Fingered Jack* that has propelled my interest in how the fantastic is mobilized in depictions of the Caribbean.

There are many more avenues that this project could have pursued. For example, there is the portrayal of Afro-Caribbean practices in popular television series such as *American Horror Story*. Additionally, expanding the range of sources to include more texts from the non-English-speaking Caribbean would have enhanced the foundation of the book's arguments. For example, exploring the work of the Cuban sci-fi writer Yoss would have provided a compelling supplement to my discussion of Buckell's work. Despite these limitations, *Working Juju* closes with a final example that demonstrates the book's argument that the deployment of the fantastic from within the region most often serves to critique the region's legacy of imperialism and internal deterioration, whereas its activation from agents external to the region in both geography and cultural affiliation often pathologizes the region and distracts attention from the ravaging effects of slavery and the colonial project.

APPENDIX

Interview with Tobias Buckell

AN: What is the first book you remember reading, and how did your early reading experiences shape you as both a reader and a writer?

TB: I have vague memories of kids' books when I was learning to read. I remember giving my teacher's assistant in prekindergarten *The Billy Goats Gruff* and making her read it to me over and over again. I was obsessed with unlocking the puzzle of what those markings on the page and all around me meant, like older people could. And once I learned the basics, I remember just going hard at trying to advance up the ladder to more and more complicated books. I didn't want simple picture books. I wanted to read the big things, like adults. At the library in St. George's in Grenada, I kept sneaking off into the adult section and getting put back in the kid's. So the first proper adult book, the first "proper" book in my young mind, was Clive Cussler's *Raise the Titanic*! My mom had it lying around, and I picked it up and read it. After I proved myself, she started letting me read novels after her, a lot of techno-thrillers and spy novels. So I've always really enjoyed fast action.

    The big experience that changed my life was finding a copy of *Childhood's End*, by Arthur C. Clarke, in the library of my dad's boat that he used to shuttle tourists to beaches. It blew my mind. I didn't understand a fraction of it, but I knew that I wanted more of whatever that was. I was between seven and ten. It altered the trajectory of my life and started my love of all things science fictional.

AN: What are you reading now?

TB: Fiction: I just got *Infomacracy* by Malka Older to start reading later this evening.

    Non-fiction: I am halfway through *Tools of Titans* by Tim Ferriss.

AN: Where do you most associate with the idea of "home," and what does home mean to you?

TB: That's a tough one. I moved around so much when I was young, and because I lived on a boat, it's only been recently that I've started to form a concept of home itself now that I've spent fifteen years in the same town in Ohio. Ijeoma Umebinyuo said, "So, here you / too foreign for home / too foreign for here. Never enough for both." That quote knocked me off my seat. I feel that even though I have white-looking skin and can blend in where I live now, I feel much the same. An in-between sort of person. I think home for me is the amalgamation of my memories and relationships from both Grenada and the Virgin Islands. I know that when I go to the southernmost islands, I feel like I'm "back." It's a combination of the "cree cree" of the tree frogs as dusk hits, the smell of the wind, the taste of the roti, the way people sound, the contacts I have. When I visit places like Barbados or Trinidad, I suddenly want to belong and feel a strong yearning. Is that home? Do people who have home also feel that even as they yearn, their time away means that they're always going to be just one step to the side because home is also a specific time, not just a place, and it has long since passed you by, since you weren't there anymore? There's the phrase "stranger in a strange land," but I often feel like a "stranger in a comfortably familiar land" no matter where I am.

AN: Have you ever considered returning to live in the Caribbean? Why would this be or not be ideal for you?

TB: I've thought about it a lot. I can't afford the real estate right now. I might live in the U.S., but I live in a very small town with super-affordable real estate and very low food prices and a very good school system. This lets me make a living as a writer, and creatives have very irregular income flows. A prominent Caribbean writer had a very interesting critique of writers who leave the Caribbean in an article I read recently, and the point they made was that the Caribbean they were writing about was one that had moved on to somewhere else.

That was one of the reasons that kept me terrified about writing Caribbean elements into my SF, a realization that made me feel like I'd betrayed my roots by moving away. But I think a lot of people realize how much diaspora goes on. I'm not the only one in this in-between space. I never turn down a reason to go back, though. And I hope against all hope that I can one day find a way to spend more and more time on an island. The long periods away feel very unmooring.

AN: In his 1972 essay "On the Poetics of the Science Fiction Genre," Darko Suvin explains sci-fi as "a literary genre whose necessary and sufficient conditions are the presence and interaction of estrangement and cognition, and whose main formal device is an imaginative framework alternative to the author's empirical environment."[1] Is this definition suitable for Caribbean sci-fi?

TB: I don't know if that would describe other Caribbean SF writers, but it is certainly a key feature of the liminal space from which I write. I grew up on a boat, so while the islands are my roots, even as a child I lived just off the shore. The two sides of my parents are from two different histories of the Caribbean, the British and the islander. That creates boundaries outside of the families that you have to negotiate. One side of the family has generations of ties to an island, and a specific place on the island. The other side are wanderers who for several generations meandered around the entire globe. Am I someone who will be rooted, family oriented, or am I a wanderer, doomed to pull up and move on soon? Then as an immigrant to the U.S., I become an outsider who lives there while then being an outsider to the Caribbean. I feel that fuels, a., why I found science fiction to be a fit for me and, b., why the framework comes naturally to me as a language.

AN: What are some of the key features of Caribbean sci-fi that you have identified and that possibly make it unique, distinguishing it from not only North American sci-fi, but sci-fi from other developing regions?

TB: I think one of the features I notice is the recognition of power, even if the characters have it. To grow up in a smaller nation is to realize that not everyone has power, or that one has limited power to wield and it has to be spent wisely. That to be nimble is to be safe. That sometimes you aren't seen. That there are a variety of ways of interacting with power. I think often in SF/F [science fiction / fantasy] the assumption of heroism is that one will bend everything to will. It's a water some swim in that they assume it's a good thing to dominate, to win, to expand, and to colonize. In Caribbean SF, the power dynamics are not assumptions but things explored, even if the main characters are dominating. There's a respect for history, and its scars as well. To know where you're coming from is to know who you are and where you are going. Some nations believe in a form of manifest destiny, and even smaller European countries, despite deep history or being smaller powers, have a sort of European version of manifest destiny, a grand story or narrative, woven through them. I also think a lot of Caribbean SF is building stuff and mashing it up, like we all do with other things. Got oil drums left behind? We make music with that. Hear Motown on the radio? We can take something from that. How many different cultures came together in the islands? The literature reaches out similarly, I think.

AN: In what specific ways do you anticipate that Caribbean sci-fi may further distinguish itself in, say, the next few decades?

TB: The next generation is amazing. I put together an anthology for the Bermuda Department of Cultural Affairs of SF/F. Karen Lord did the anthology *New Worlds, Old Ways*. The voices in there are exciting! I think of just how far above its weight the Caribbean always punches when it gets interested in something. A small island gives us a poet who is [a] Nobel Prize winner and world-renowned. Reggae is played in a bar in Nepal. Steel pan played at Christmas concerts the world around. I can't predict how or who will do it, but it will be read around the world. I know it.

AN: Cultural critic Mark Dery coined the term "Afrofuturism" in his anthology *Flame Wars: The Discourse of Cyberculture* to reference "speculative fiction that treats African-American themes and addresses African-American concerns in the context of twentieth-century techno culture—and more generally, African-American signification that appropriates images of technology and a prosthetically enhanced future."[2] Do you consider your work and the work of other Caribbean sci-fi writers as falling under the umbrella of Afrofuturism?

TB: I see it as labeled like that often. I see African writers being labeled as Afrofuturist as well, and some African writers/thinkers have run with the label. But I do think there are some key differences between the African American experience and the Caribbean experience that, despite tremendous places of overlap, don't fit together, and this affects the fiction.

While African Americans and people of the Caribbean have a common history of enslavement and the horrors and history that came with it, I think there are divergences in history that mean Caribbean SF doesn't quite fit under that umbrella at all times. The Caribbean islands are often independent nations. That means Caribbean education systems give Caribbean history, in a way African Americans don't get in a white-dominated U.S. history system. The oppressions in the islands run along different verticals than the ones in the U.S. or Europe. So a writer who comes from a free nation of mostly black people who teach a history is different in some cultural ways than the folk from a nation of white-dominated folk who go to long lengths to hide their history while contributing sometimes passively and others actively to a larger system that still very actively works against black lives.

While the Caribbean has many great issues facing it, and oppression isn't gone, nor are race relations magically sunny, the Caribbean has a number of nations in it coming from a history of enslavement, then colonialism and oppression, that resisted and fought for freedom and attained some measure of self-determination, who are looking to find their way forward in a complicated world. The Afrofuturists in the U.S. are members of a class people still engaged in active resistance and negotiation in a mostly oppressive society. The fiction from each of those situations is different.

However, the caveat is that the diaspora means that many folk from the Caribbean leave one situation and enter the other, and vice versa. Therefore, the fiction is a "fellow traveler," and I can understand why U.S. critics will look at Caribbean fiction and see it from the lens of Afrofuturism, as it kinda looks like it, due to the commonalities. And yet I would venture a guess that some of the confusion and many of the misses that U.S. critics have when facing Caribbean SF comes from the fact that it is not Afrofuturism by strict definition.

I myself am honored when someone who is an Afrofuturist or African American labels my work as Afrofuturism. That is because I can hope that they are responding to any commonalities they sense between the two currents. But when someone from outside of Afrofuturism or the African American experience uses the label, I feel it's at risk of missing something important and too hastily applied. That may not seem fair to that outsider, but that doesn't stop making it true for me.

AN: In the introduction to the anthology *So Long Been Dreaming: Postcolonial Science Fiction and Fantasy*, Nalo Hopkinson observes the irony that sci-fi "speaks so much about the experience of being alienated, but contains so little written by alienated people themselves."[3] How might you respond to Hopkinson's observation?

TB: She's so damn right! It's often, "Let's go colonize this planet," but we have fewer stories where the earth gets colonized and everyone's like, "Oh shit, what do we do now? How do you resist this?" And in the crappy mode of resistance in a lot of SF—like, think, *Independence Day*—it becomes a story of the plucky Earthlings who just rise up and kick ass. You see that in white males who write about slavery; it's always a character-building arc in the fiction for them. Someone's a slave, but they kick ass at it, and it's not really any worse than being a blue-collar worker. Then they revolt and win. It ignores the brutality of slavery and colonization in those stories and how hard and infrequent successful revolts were. The U.S. writers map the U.S. Revolution onto slavery and seem to suggest, "If we had been slaves, we'd have risen up" or "If I'd been a slave, I'd have kicked ass and been out of the situation after the hard work buffed me up."

There's so little counternarrative to this. And there needs to be, because as a society, this narrative slowly seeps in and gives the message "They deserved to be oppressed because they were complacent about it. If someone tried to do that to us, we wouldn't have stood for it." I find it corrosive.

AN: What has been the most memorable response to your work from a Caribbean reader?

TB: You love the moments where people freak out to meet you, of course, but my favorite experience was an islander who wrote a review of my first book and said that it wasn't exotic to them. If they wanted to go outside to the bush, they'd step out into their backyard, and if they wanted to read about the food in their kitchen, they'd just get up and go eat it. They wanted to go somewhere truly alien! That "meh" review meant the world to me, as it meant I'd nailed the flavor for that person, who felt that made it too familiar. I was so proud, I printed that out for my wall for a long time.

AN: Do you have any plans to develop a new series of Caribbean-esque novels? If so, is there anything you can tell us about the universe in which these novels will be set or the plot that will drive the series?

TB: Someone I trust once read one of my short story collections and pointed out to me that they could see the Caribbean influence in all the stories, even the nonobviously Caribbean ones. I have a story coming out in an anthology in April that's about a robot that maintains a starship hull. In some ways, the setting is classic big-idea space opera SF. But the character, the idea for the story, the resonance in it, all came from my reading about work-resistance strategies of pre-independent Caribbean islands. It's one of the most Caribbean things I've written, as far as its inception. Yet it won't seem that way to most.

I'm starting a new fantasy novel. I have no idea what it will look like by completion, but I'm willing to bet the islands are laced throughout. I'm trying not to second-guess myself but just throw myself into the writing and see what comes of it.

AN: In an article titled "A Working Model for Analyzing Third World Science Fiction: The Case of Brazil," M. Elizabeth Ginway argues that "science fiction written in the Third World requires critical tools different from those typically applied to European and Anglo-American sf, because the shift in geographical and cultural contexts can force a reinterpretation of the genre's basic premises."[4] She further explains: "In my search for an approach to science fiction in Brazil, I found a consideration of cultural myths to provide an excellent point of departure because, as we shall see, they are evoked by early sf writers and often satirized by contemporary ones." She offers examples of cultural myths such as "Brazil as a green, tropical paradise; Brazil as a racial democracy; Brazilians as a sensual and non-violent people; and Brazil as a country with potential for national greatness or *grandeza*, as well for its shadow side, *malandragem*." Which cultural myths about the Caribbean might you identify as a suitable "point of departure" for discussing your work and the work of other Caribbean sci-fi writers?

TB: The touchstone for most is tourism. Beaches, rum punch, "hey mon" —I twitch whenever I see the word "mon"—weed and hotels and sun. A lot of assumptions about capacity—people are very dismissive of smaller countries. I get letters from angry white SF readers who lecture me that Caribbean folk don't have the technical capacity to get to space. It's not something they equate with vacationland.

    I know that these premises hobble my ability to be taken seriously by many in my chosen field. My first story to be chosen for a *Year's Best* collection was "Toy Planes." It's the story of the first Caribbean launch to space of an experimental rocket plane. When I read it in the islands, it gets a very strong reaction. It's something of a mission statement for me, why I am writing much of my fiction. It's an emotional story; people tear up. But when I got my copies of the *Year's Best* it was in, the introduction, by a much-esteemed editor in the field with a great deal of influence, read something like "This a fun, cute, very short little story." It was a punch to the gut. I knew this was happening, but here it was confirmed in black-and-white.

    I pack that in my furnace and use it to fuel my rage to continue on, no matter what. My goal is to someday be so good I can't be ignored. There's a long road ahead of me, but I'm committed.

AN: Your novels seem to eschew religion, situating it as the cause of irrational and unsavory behavior and, in many ways, the basis of the much of the tragedy experienced by your characters. If you don't mind sharing, what are your personal religious views, and have these influenced how you situate religion in your writing?

TB: I don't know if I set out to show it was irrational so much as that religion is often a weapon wielded against us. Slaveholders quoted biblical passages to justify slavery. Today people are told that oppressive politics that work for the 1 percent are what Jesus would have wanted, when it looks pretty clear he wasn't a fan of accumulation of wealth.

As a result, I felt very sympathetic to Oaxyctl's situation in *Crystal Rain*. In *Sly Mongoose*, I tried to show how the religion had suffered through the reveal of its gods as manipulative aliens, and yet the core organic religion adapted and remained a background presence for descendants.

I have this sort of ambivalent relationship with religion in that I view it as a tool. When younger, it was often wielded against me, so I do tend to have a stronger interest in poking around its negative uses. However, I'm also fascinated by the people who use it as a tool against oppression: usually the original founders of a major religion, as well as figures like MLK and the people behind movements like Moral Mondays. Because religion is a dominant narrative in most modern societies, I don't think justice will be found, or oppression fought, unless using religion, because it uses the language of the oppressor. I'm still beginning to play with some of those themes, however.

NOTES

INTRODUCTION. Kingdoms in Other Worlds

1. Mighty Sparrow, "Obeah Wedding," track B2 on *Calypso Genius Vol. 1*, National Recording Company, 1966, 33⅓ rpm.

2. Edward Long, *The History of Jamaica; or, General Survey of the Antient and Modern State of the Island, with Reflections on Its Situation, Settlements, Inhabitants, Climate, Products, Commerce, Laws, and Government*, 3 vols. (London: T. Lowndes, 1774), 2:416.

3. Giselle Anatol, *The Things That Fly in the Night* (New Brunswick, N.J.: Rutgers University Press, 2015), 1; the other quotations from Anatol in this paragraph are from pages 3–4, 19, and 21–22.

4. Joan Dayan, *Haiti, History, and the Gods* (Berkeley: University of California Press, 1996), 265.

5. Ibid.

6. Mimi Sheller, *Consuming the Caribbean: From Arawaks to Zombies* (New York: Routledge, 2003), 3.

7. Jacques Derrida, *Specters of Marx: The State of the Debt, the Work of Mourning, and the New International*, trans. Peggy Kamuf (New York: Routledge, 1994). Subsequent quotations and references in this paragraph to Derrida's work come from page xviii.

8. Michael Dash, *Haiti and the United States: National Stereotypes and the Literary Imagination* (New York: Springer, 2016), 6–7; the other quotations from Dash in this paragraph are from pages 10 and 23.

9. Mimi Sheller contends that European allegations of cannibalism among Amerindians in the Caribbean selectively vilified indigenous group like the Caribs, who rebelled against colonization (*Consuming the Caribbean*, 148). Sheller cites Lola Young's *Fear of the Dark: 'Race,' Gender, and Sexuality in the Cinema* (London: Routledge, 1996), which

145

suggests that these accusations helped justify Europe's barbaric behavior in the New World.

10. "Cannibals in Hayti," *Harper's Magazine*, Sept. 2, 1865, 545.

11. Robert Lawless, *Haiti's Bad Press* (Cambridge, Mass.: Schenkman, 1992), xiii.

12. Quoted in ibid., 34.

13. Hans Schmidt, *The United States Occupation of Haiti, 1915–1934* (New Brunswick, N.J., Rutgers University Press, 1971), 42. Schmidt indicates that between 1888 and 1915, ten of the country's eleven presidents were murdered or unseated by insurgents.

14. Ibid., 42–56.

15. Sarah Lauro, *The TransAtlantic Zombie: Slavery, Rebellion, and Living Death* (New Brunswick, N.J.: Rutgers University Press, 2015), 14.

16. Joan Dayan, *Vodoun, or the Voice of the Gods* (New Brunswick: N.J., Rutgers University Press, 1991), 33.

17. Ibid., 33.

18. Dash, *Haiti and the United States*, 25, 24.

19. William Seabrook, *The Magic Island* (New York: Harcourt, Brace, 1929; Mineola, N.Y.: Dover, 2016), 62. Citations refer to the Dover edition.

20. Danny Shea, "Pat Robertson: Haiti 'Cursed' by 'Pact to the Devil'" *Huffington Post*, Mar. 18, 2010, updated Dec. 6, 2017, https://www.huffingtonpost.com/2010/01/13/pat-robertson-haiti-curse_n_422099.html.

21. Albert Mohler, "Does God Hate Haiti?" *Washington Post*, Jan. 20, 2010.

22. Some noteworthy patterns are associated with generative myths about Caribbean sovereignty. For example, the national flower of Bermuda is said to have grown from the ashes of a murdered slave; the ritual performed by the Vodun priest Dutty Boukman heralded the Haitian Revolution by promising protection to the slaves; and stories of the Jamaican national hero and Maroon leader Queen Nanny allege that she could catch bullets with her buttocks. A similarly fantastical event that occurred in Cuba in response to colonial oppression is known as "La Luz de Yara" (the Light of Yara). Yvette Fuentes, a scholar of the Caribbean and Latin America explains: "Yara is a little town between Bayamo and Manzanillo and it was where the native cacique Taino Hatuey was burned at the stake by the Spaniards in the sixteenth century. The town is also important because it was there that the first call for independence from Spain took place in 1868 (first war of independence). According to the legend, a mysterious light appears to people before an important event and they say it is the soul of Hatuey" (personal communication with the author, Apr. 5, 2015).

23. C. L. R. James, *The Black Jacobins: Toussaint L'Ouverture and the San Domingo Revolution* (London: Secker & Warburg, 1938; London: Penguin, 2001), 117. Citations refer to the Penguin edition. According to Merriam Webster online, wanga is "voodoo sorcery; also: a voodooistic charm or spell."

24. Schmidt, *Occupation of Haiti*, 22, 23.

25. Alejo Carpentier, *The Kingdom of This World: A Novel*, trans. Harriet De Onís (1949; repr., New York: Macmillan, 2006), 86–87.

26. Ibid.

27. Margarite Fernandez Olmos and Lizabeth Paravisini-Gebert, *Creole Religions of the Caribbean: An Introduction from Vodou and Santería to Obeah and Espiritismo* (New York: NYU Press, 2011), 16.

28. Ibid., 103.

29. Mary Reckord, "The Jamaica Slave Rebellion of 1831," *Past & Present* 40 (July 1968): 108.

30. Diana Paton, *The Cultural Politics of Obeah: Religion, Colonialism, and Modernity in the Caribbean World* (Cambridge: Cambridge University Press, 2015), 65; the other quotation in this paragraph from Paton is also from page 65.

31. Kenneth Bilby, "An (Un)natural Mystic in the Air: Images of Obeah in Caribbean Song," in *Obeah and Other Powers: The Politics of Caribbean Religion and Healing*, ed. Diana Paton and Maarit Forde (Durham, N.C.: Duke University Press, 2012), 50.

32. Mighty Sparrow, "Witch Doctor," on *Dance Party Gold*, BLS Records, June 30, 1994, compact disc.

33. Owen Davies, *Grimoires: A History of Magic Books* (Oxford: Oxford University Press, 2010). Information about de Laurence in this paragraph comes from pages 215–16.

34. Ibid., 220. Information about de Laurence in this paragraph comes from pages 217, 222, and 227.

35. Lauron William de Laurence, *The Sixth and Seventh Books of Moses: The Mystery of All Mysteries. The Citation on All Spirits, the Spirit in the Burning Bush, "Helmet of Moses and Aaron," Healing by Amulets. The Wonderful Magical and Spirit Arts of Moses and Aaron, and the Old Wise Hebrews, Taken from the Mosaic Books for the Good of Mankind* (Chicago: De Laurence, Scott, 1910).

36. Patrick Polk, *Other Books, Other Powers: "The 6th and 7th Books of Moses" in Afro-Atlantic Folk Belief* (Lexington: University Press of Kentucky, 1999), 120.

37. Davies, *Grimoires*, 224. Additional information from *Grimoires* in this paragraph comes from pages 227–30.

38. Jamaica Customs Agency, "Prohibited Items," 2018, https://www.jacustoms.gov.jm/service/prohibited-items.

39. Polk, *Other Books, Other Powers*, 216.

40. Davies, *Grimoires*, 216.

41. Philip Deslippe, "The Hindu in Hoodoo: Fake Yogis, Pseudo-Swamis, and the Manufacture of African American Folk Magic," *Amerasia Journal* 40, no. 1 (2014): 39. The other quotation from Deslippe in this paragraph is from page 41.

42. Polk, *Other Books, Other Powers*, 128. The second quotation from Polk in this paragraph is from the same page.

43. Merriam-Webster online, s.vv. "paranormal" and "supernatural."

44. Marek Oziewicz, "Speculative Fiction," *Oxford Research Encyclopedia of Literature*, Mar. 2017, http://literature.oxfordre.com/view/10.1093/acrefore/9780190201098 .001.0001/acrefore-9780190201098-e-78.

45. Tzvetan Todorov, *The Fantastic: A Structural Approach to a Literary Genre* (Cleveland: Case Western Reserve University Press, 1973), 33; the following quotation in this paragraph is from page 25.

46. Merriam-Webster online, s.v. "magical realism."

47. Scott Simpkins, *Magical Strategies: The Supplement of Realism* (Durham, N.C.: Duke University Press, 1988), 141.

48. Alejo Carpentier, "On the Marvelous Real in America" (1949), in *Magical Realism: Theory, History, Community*, ed. Lois Zamora and Wendy Faris (Durham, N.C.: Duke University Press, 1995), 86.

49. Ibid., 84.

50. Ibid., 85, 86.

51. Stephen Slemon, "Magic Realism as Post-Colonial Discourse," *Canadian Literature* 116 (1988): 9.

52. Mda Zakes, "Acceptance Speech for the Olive Schreiner Prize," *English Academy Review* 14 (1997): 281.

CHAPTER ONE. British Obeah

Epigraph: Simon Gikandi, *Slavery and the Culture of Taste* (Princeton, N.J.: Princeton University Press, 2011).

1. Jerome S. Handler and Kenneth M. Bilby, "On the Early Use and Origin of the Term 'Obeah' in Barbados and the Anglophone Caribbean," *Slavery and Abolition* 22 (2001): 87.

2. Alan Richardson, "Romantic Voodoo: Obeah and British Culture, 1797–1807," in *Sacred Possessions: Vodou, Santería, Obeah, and the Caribbean*, ed. Margarite Fernández Olmos and Lizabeth Paravisini-Gebert (New Brunswick, N.J.: Rutgers University Press, 1997), 179, 190.

3. Lizabeth Paravisini-Gebert, "Colonial and Postcolonial Gothic," in *The Cambridge Companion to Gothic Fiction*, ed. Jerrold E. Hogle (Cambridge: Cambridge University Press 2002), 229–258.

4. Diana Paton, *The Cultural Politics of Obeah: Religion, Colonialism, and Modernity in the Caribbean World* (Cambridge: Cambridge University Press, 2015), 47.

5. Edward Long, *The History of Jamaica; or, General Survey of the Antient and Modern State of the Island, with Reflections on Its Situation, Settlements, Inhabitants, Climate, Products, Commerce, Laws, and Government*, 3 vols. (London: T. Lowndes, 1774), 2:409.

6. Ibid., 2:416–22; quotation on 416.

7. Bryan Edwards, *The History, Civil and Commercial, of the British Colonies in the West Indies* (London: Stockdale, 1794), 2:296.

8. Matthew Gregory Lewis, *Journal of a West-India Proprietor, Kept during a Residence in the Island of Jamaica* (London: Murray, 1834), 138.

9. James Anthony Froude, *The English in the West Indies; or, The Bow of Ulysses* (London: Longmans, Green, 1888), 126.

10. Richardson, "Romantic Voodoo," 173.

11. Margarite Fernández Olmos and Lizabeth Paravisini-Gebert, *Creole Religions of the Caribbean: An Introduction from Vodou and Santería to Obeah and Espiritismo* (New York: NYU Press, 2011), 103.

12. Richardson, "Romantic Voodoo," 173; Olmos and Paravisini-Gebert, *Creole Religions of the Caribbean*, 103.

13. Olmos and Paravisini-Gebert, *Creole Religions of the Caribbean*, 103.

14. Celucien Joseph, "The Rhetoric of Prayer: Dutty Boukman, the Discourse of 'Freedom from Below,' and the Politics of God," *Journal of Race, Ethnicity, and Religion* 2, no. 9 (2011): 5.

15. Olmos and Paravisini-Gebert, *Creole Religions of the Caribbean*, 15.

16. Walter Rucker, "Conjure, Magic, and Power: The Influence of Afro-Atlantic Religious Practices on Slave Resistance and Rebellion," *Journal of Black Studies* 32, no. 1 (2001): 87.

17. Richardson, "Romantic Voodoo," 173.

18. Dorothy Hammond and Alta Jablow, *The Africa That Never Was* (New York: Twayne, 1970; Long Grove, Ill.: Waveland, 1992). Citations are to the Waveland edition.

19. Michel-Rolph Trouillot, *Global Transformations, Anthropology, and the Modern World* (London: Palgrave Macmillan, 2016), 12, 15, 19, 18; quotations on 12 and 18.

20. Paton and Forde, introduction to *Obeah and Other Powers*, 26.

21. Sylvia Wynter, "Columbus, the Ocean Blue, and Fables That Stir the Mind: To Reinvent the Study of Letters," in *Poetics of the Americas: Race, Founding, and Textuality*, ed. Bainard Cowan and Jefferson Humphries (Baton Rouge: Louisiana State University Press, 1997), 153.

22. Paget Henry, *Caliban's Reason: Introducing Afro-Caribbean Philosophy* (London: Routledge, 2002), 74, 75, 77.

23. Abdul R. JanMohamed, "The Economy of Manichean Allegory: The Function of

Racial difference in Colonialist Literature," *Critical Inquiry* 12, no. 1 (1985): 81; all quotations are from this page.

24. Ibid., 84, 86.

25. Edwards, *British Colonies in the West Indies*, 2:299.

26. Lewis, *Journal of a West-India Proprietor*, 149, 150.

27. Ibid., 146.

28. Edwards, *British Colonies in the West Indies*, 2:295, 296.

29. Long, *History of Jamaica*, 2:420.

30. Ibid., 2:418.

31. William Earle, *Obi; or, The History of Three-Fingered Jack*, ed. Srinivas Aravamudan (Peterborough, Ont.: Broadview, 2005), 10, 13.

32. Ibid., 14, 15.

33. Ibid., 115, 156; quotation on 156.

34. Paton, *Cultural Politics of Obeah*, 72.

35. Rucker, "Conjure, Magic, and Power," 84.

36. Randy M. Browne, "The "'Bad Business' of Obeah: Power, Authority, and the Politics of Slave Culture in the British Caribbean," *William and Mary Quarterly* 68, no. 3 (2011): 455, 456.

37. John Savage, "'Black Magic' and White Terror: Slave Poisoning and Colonial Society in Early 19th Century Martinique," *Journal of Social History* 40, no. 3 (2007): 636, 637, 639; quotations on 636 and 639.

38. Rucker, "Conjure, Magic, and Power," 86.

39. Elsa V. Goveia, *A Study on the Historiography of the British West Indies* (Mexico City: Pan American Institute of History and Geography, 1956), 248.

40. Ibid., 61, 62.

41. Paton, *Cultural Politics of Obeah*, 1; the other quotation from Paton in this paragraph is from page 57.

42. Simon Gikandi, *Slavery and the Culture of Taste* (Princeton, N.J.: Princeton University Press, 2011), 259, 263, 262, 260; quotations on 259 and 260.

43. Ibid., 261, 269; quotation on 261.

44. Paton, *Cultural Politics of Obeah*, 69.

45. Nana Wilson-Tagoe, *The Scope and Limits of West Indian Historiography: Historical Thought and Literary Representation in West Indian Literature* (Melton, UK: James Currey, 1998), 16, 17.

46. Ibid., 18, 19.

47. Paton, *Cultural Politics of Obeah*, 69.

48. Faith Smith, *Creole Recitations: John Jacob Thomas and Colonial Formation in the Late Nineteenth-Century Caribbean* (New Brunswick, N.J.: Rutgers University Press, 2002), 10.

49. Lara Putnam, "Rites of Power and Rumors of Race: The Circulation of Supernatural Knowledge in the Greater Caribbean, 1890–1940," in Paton and Forde, *Obeah and Other Powers*, 256.

50. Wilson Harris, "History, Fable and Myth in the Caribbean and Guianas," *Caribbean Quarterly*, 16, no. 2 (1970): 7.

51. Wilson-Tagoe, *West Indian Historiography*, 22, 23.

CHAPTER TWO. Devilish Divas and Gangster Monsters

Epigraph: Stuart Hall, "When Was 'the Post-Colonial'? Thinking at the Limit," in *The Postcolonial Question: Common Skies, Divided Horizons*, ed. Iain Chambers and Lidia Curti (London: Routledge, 1996), 259.

1. Sidney Wilfred Mintz, *Caribbean Transformations* (New York: Columbia University Press, 2007), 49.

2. Michael Richardson, *Otherness in Hollywood Cinema* (New York: Continuum, 2010), 49.

3. Julia Kristeva, *Powers of Horror: An Essay on Abjection*, trans. Leon S. Rudiez (New York: Columbia University Press, 1982), 4.

4. Leonard Cassuto, *The Inhuman Race: The Racial Grotesque in American Literature and Culture* (New York: Columbia University Press, 1997), 8.

5. Laura Mulvey, "Visual Pleasure and Narrative Cinema," in *Visual and Other Pleasures* (Houndmills, UK: Palgrave Macmillan, 1989).

6. Joan Dayan, *Haiti, History, and the Gods* (Berkeley: University of California Press, 1996), 265.

7. Bliss Cua Lim, *Translating Time: Cinema, the Fantastic, and Temporal Critique* (Durham, N.C.: Duke University Press, 2009), 13–14, 12; McClintock quoted on 13–14.

8. Ed Guerrero, *Framing Blackness: The African American Image in Film* (Philadelphia: Temple University Press, 1993), 56–57.

9. Adilifu Nama, *Black Space: Imagining Race in Science Fiction Film* (Austin: University of Texas Press, 2010), 2.

10. Joshua David Bellin, *Framing Monsters: Fantasy Film and Social Alienation* (Carbondale: Southern Illinois University Press, 2005), 2, 13; the other quotations from Bellin come from page 13.

11. Chet Van Duzer, "Hic Sunt Dracones: The Geography and Cartography of Monsters," in *The Ashgate Research Companion to Monsters and the Monstrous*, ed. Asa Simon Mittman and Peter Dendle (Farnham, UK: Ashgate, 2012), 391.

12. Persephone Braham, "The Monstrous Caribbean," in Mittman and Dandel, *Monsters and the Monstrous*, 17.

13. Bellin, *Framing Monsters*, 15, 13, 1; quotations on 13 and 1.

14. Guerrero, *Framing Blackness*, 43.

15. Milton Vickerman situates Caribbean films in three categories, including "Paradoxical Islands: Beauty and Danger." He argues that "from the very beginning, Whites exhibited starkly divergent responses towards the West Indies; at once attracted by its physical beauty and the opportunities which it provided but repelled by the sometimes harsh climate and the perceived hostility of its inhabitants" (Vickerman, "Representing West Indians in Film: Ciphers, Coons, and Criminals," *Western Journal of Black Studies* 23, no. 2 [1999]: 86–87). According to Vickerman, films within this category are likely to represent the Caribbean as either paradisial or horrific. I argue that some fantasy and horror films, such as the *Pirates of the Caribbean* series and numerous zombie films, present the region as both, and that this conflicted filmic portrayal is replicated by the main characters' relationship with the Caribbean.

16. Isaiah Lavender uses the term "blackground" in relation to science fiction literature, but here I am appropriating its use for film; see Lavender, *Race in American Science Fiction* (Bloomington: Indiana University Press, 2011), 6.

17. John Rieder, *Colonialism and the Emergence of Science Fiction* (Middleton, Conn.: Wesleyan University Press, 2008), 4.

18. V. S. Naipaul, *Miguel Street* 1.

19. K. Q. Warner, *On Location: Cinema and Film in the Anglophone Caribbean* (London: Macmillan, 2000), 8.

20. Ibid., 31, 28, 36.

21. Desmond Dekker, "007 Shanty Town"; video posted to YouTube by Eric Cajundelyon, Jan. 24, 2013, https://www.youtube.com/watch?v=ZqgWuMcHc3g.

22. Website of Rose Hall Developments, https://rosehall.com.

23. The exact figures are $1,066,200,000 for *Dead Man's Chest* and $963,400,000 for *At World's End*; see "All Time Box Office" at Box Office Mojo, https://www.boxofficemojo.com/alltime/world.

24. Margarite Fernández Olmos and Lizabeth Paravisini-Gebert, *Creole Religions of the Caribbean: An Introduction from Vodou and Santería to Obeah and Espiritismo* (New York: NYU Press, 2011), 154, 157.

25. M. Kuumba and Femi Ajanaku, "Dreadlocks: The Hair Aesthetics of Cultural Resistance and Collective Identity Formation," *Mobilization* 3, no. 2 (October 1998): 227–43.

26. Kevin Frank suggests that the pirates in the *Pirates of the Caribbean* movies are adorned with dreadlocks as a "way of suggesting the dehumanized and fearful lives they lead as cursed souls" (Frank, "Whether Beast or Human: The Cultural Legacies of Dread, Locks, and Dystopia," *Small Axe* 11, no. 2 [June 2007]: 60). While I agree that Hollywood often invokes locks to infer deviance and is likely doing so in this case,

I think that Sparrow's locks function in tandem with other elements of his persona, like his stride and his gestures, to signal his iconoclastic status.

27. Anne Petersen, "'You Believe in Pirates, of Course . . .': Disney's Commodification and 'Closure' vs. Johnny Depp's Aesthetic Piracy of 'Pirates of the Caribbean,'" *Studies in Popular Culture* 29, no. 2 (2007): 63–81.

28. Jessica Diehl and Patti Smith, "The Crowded Mind of Johnny Depp," *Vanity Fair*, Dec. 27, 2010, https://www.vanityfair.com/news/2011/01/johnny-depp-201101.

29. Erin Skye Mackie, "Welcome the Outlaw: Pirates, Maroons, and Caribbean Countercultures," *Cultural Critique* 59, no. 1 (2005): 24–62.

30. Mintz, *Caribbean Transformations*, 45.

31. Bolster also explains that blacks worked as seamen in other capacities than as pirates. Some even held positions as pilots and sea captains, commanding white crew members; see W. Jeffrey Bolster, *Black Jacks: African American Seamen in the Age of Sail* (Cambridge, Mass.: Harvard University Press, 2009), 132–33.

32. Mackie, "Welcome the Outlaw," 24, 26.

33. Sebastian Clarke, *The Evolution of Popular Jamaican Song* (London: Heinemann, 1980), 111.

34. Quoted in ibid., 112.

35. Alfred Métraux, *Voodoo in Haiti*, trans. and ed. Hugo Charteris (1958; New York: Schocken, 1972), 110, 112.

36. Sir Henry Bell, who lived in Grenada during the late nineteenth century, observed the practice of hanging "Obeah bottles"; see Henry Hesketh Bell, *Obeah: Witchcraft in the West Indies*, 2nd ed. (London: Sampson Low, Marston, 1893), 16.

37. Kameelah Martin Samuel, "Disney's Tia Dalma: A Critical Interrogation of an 'Imagineered' Priestess," *Black Women, Gender & Families* 6, no. 1 (2012): 100.

38. Beth Allcock, "Not Just a Bond Girl: Who is Naomie Harris?," *Sun*, Apr. 13, 2018, https://www.thesun.co.uk/tvandshowbiz/2450253/naomie-harris-moneypenny-james-bond-pirates-of-the-caribbean-chiwetel-ejiofor.

39. Frank, "Whether Beast or Human," 59.

40. Samuel, "Disney's Tia Dalma," 99.

41. Homer, *The Odyssey of Homer*, trans. Richmond Lattimore (New York: Harper & Row, 1965), 117, 118.

42. bell hooks, "Selling Hot Pussy: Representations of Black Female Sexuality in the Cultural Marketplace," in *Black Looks: Race and Representation* (London: Turnaround, 1992), 115, 117.

43. Barbara Creed, *The Monstrous-Feminine: Film, Feminism, Psychoanalysis* (Abingdon, UK: Routledge, 1993), 7.

44. Christopher Columbus, "Letter from Columbus to Luis de Santangel," Feb. 15,

1493, 268, American Journeys Collection, document AJ-063, Wisconsin Historical Society Digital Library and Archives, 2003, americanjourneys.org/aj-063/index.asp.

45. Edward Said, *Orientalism* (New York: Vintage, 1979).

46. Samuel, "Disney's Tia Dalma," 110.

47. Sarah J. Lauro, *The Transatlantic Zombie: Slavery, Rebellion, and Living Death* (Brunswick, N.J.: Rutgers University Press, 2015), 13.

48. Ann Kordas, "New South, New Immigrants, New Women, New Zombies," in *Race, Oppression, and the Zombie: Essays on Cross-Cultural Appropriations of the Caribbean Tradition*, ed. Christopher M. Moreman and Cory James Rushton (Jefferson, N.C.: McFarland, 2011), 15.

49. Peter Dendle, "The Zombie as Barometer of Cultural Anxiety," in *Monsters and the Monstrous: Myths and Metaphors of Enduring Evil* (New York: Amsterdam, 2007), 6.

50. Ibid., 49.

51. Shawn McIntosh, "The Evolution of the Zombie: The Monster That Keeps Coming Back," in *Zombie Culture: Autopsies of the Living Dead*, ed. Shawn McIntosh and Marc Leverette (Lanham, Md.: Scarecrow, 2008), 5.

52. Dayan, *Haiti, History, and the Gods*, 37.

53. Dendle, "Zombie as Barometer," 45.

54. Elizabeth Young, "Here Comes the Bride: Wedding, Gender, and Race in 'Bride of Frankenstein,'" *Feminist Studies* 17, no. 3 (1991): 403–37.

55. Chera Kee, "'They Are Not Men . . . They are Dead Bodies': From Cannibal to Zombie and Back Again," in *Better Off Dead: The Evolution of the Zombie as Post-Human*, ed. Deborah Christie and Sarah Juliet Lauro (New York: Fordham University Press, 2011), 15.

56. Wade Dave, *Passage of Darkness: The Ethnobiology of the Haitian Zombie* (Chapel Hill: University of North Carolina Press, 1988), 26.

57. Kee, "They Are Not Men," 9.

58. Jody Duncan, *The Winston Effect: The Art and History of Stan Winston Studio* (London: Titan, 2006), 336.

59. Nama, *Black Space*, 76.

60. Olmos and Paravisini-Gebert, "Creole Religions of the Caribbean," 126–27.

61. Ibid., 157.

62. Kuumba and Ajanaku, "Dreadlocks."

63. John Tehranian, "Performing Whiteness: Naturalization Litigation and the Construction of Racial Identity in America," *Yale Law Journal* 109, no. 4 (2000): 817–48.

64. Opportunity Agenda, "Power of Pop: Media Analysis of Representations of Immigrants in Popular TV Shows," The Opportunity Agenda, 2017, https://opportunityagenda.org/explore/resources-publications/power-pop/executive-summary.

65. Michelangelo Landgrave and Alex Nowrasteh, *Criminal Immigrants: Their Numbers, Demographics, and Countries of Origin* (Washington, D.C., Cato Institute, 2017), 4.

66. Laurie Gunst, *Born Fi' Dead: A Journey through the Jamaican Posse Underworld* (New York: Holt, 1995), xviii; the other quotations from Gunst in this paragraph are from pages xviii and xxii–xxiii.

67. Deborah A. Thomas, *Exceptional Violence: Embodied Citizenship in Transnational Jamaica* (Durham, N.C.: Duke University Press, 2011), 2; the other quotations from Thomas in this paragraph are from pages 2–3, 10, and 4.

CHAPTER THREE. The Haunting of a Nation

Epigraph: Wilson Harris, "Apprenticeship to the Furies," in *Selected Essays of Wilson Harris: The Unfinished Genesis of the Imagination*, ed. Andrew Bundy (London: Routledge, 2005), 218.

1. Martin Munro, *The Haunted Tropics: Caribbean Ghost Stories* (Kingston, Jamaica: University of the West Indies Press, 2015), vii.

2. Bernews, "Sally Basset and 'The Dangerous Spirit of Liberty,'" Bernews.com, Nov. 23, 2010, http://bernews.com/2010/11/sally-bassett-the-dangerous-spirit-of-liberty.

3. Thanks to my friend Antonia McDonald-Smythe for sharing this bit of information with me in a conversation on June 6, 2016.

4. "A Ghost in St. Lucia?," *Dominica News Online*, October 17, 2013, http://dominicanewsonline.com/news/homepage/news/general/ghost-st-lucia.

5. Linda Dégh, *Legend and Belief: Dialectics of a Folklore Genre* (Bloomington: Indiana University Press, 2001), 21.

6. In contrast, Merriam Webster online defines folklore as "traditional customs, beliefs, stories, and sayings" and as "ideas or stories that are not true but that many people have heard or read."

7. Dégh, *Legend and Belief*, 21.

8. Diane Goldstein, Sylvia Grider, and Jeannie Banks Thomas, *Haunting Experiences: Ghosts in Contemporary Folklore* (Boulder: University Press of Colorado, 2007), 26, 30.

9. Michiko Iwasaka and Barre Toelken, *Ghosts and the Japanese: Cultural Experience in Japan's Death Legends* (Logan: Utah State University Press, 1994), 20.

10. William L. MacDonald, "The Popularity of Paranormal Experiences in the United States," *Journal of American Culture* 17, no. 3 (1994): 35–42.

11. Gillian Bennett, *Alas, Poor Ghost! Traditions of Belief in Story and Discourse* (Logan: Utah State University Press, 1999), 14.

12. Barbara Walker, *Out of the Ordinary: Folklore and the Supernatural* (Logan: Utah State University Press, 1995), 2.

13. Cathy Caruth, *Trauma: Explorations in Memory* (Baltimore: Johns Hopkins University Press, 1995), 4; second quotation on page 5.

14. Saidiya Hartman, *Lose Your Mother: A Journey along the Atlantic Slave Route* (New York: Farrar, Straus and Giroux, 2008), 86; other quoted material from this author is on pages 86 and 85. Elmina Castle was a fort in Ghana where captured Africans were held before being shipped to the Americas during the transatlantic slave trade.

15. Ian Baucom, *Specters of the Atlantic: Finance Capital, Slavery, and the Philosophy of History* (Durham, N.C.: Duke University Press, 2001), 63.

16. Achille Mbembe, "Necropolitics," trans. Libby Meintjes, *Public Culture* 15, no. 1 (2003): 11.

17. Vincent Brown, *The Reaper's Garden: Death and Power in the World of Atlantic Slavery* (Cambridge, Mass.: Harvard University Press, 2008), 5; other quotations from Brown in this paragraph are from pages 5, 6, and 65.

18. John S. Mbiti, *African Religions and Philosophy*, 2nd ed. (Oxford: Heinemann, 1990), xi; subsequent references to and quotations from Mbiti in this paragraph come from pages 83, 84, and 79.

19. Brown, *Reaper's Garden*, 65; subsequent quotations from Brown in this paragraph come from pages 65, 70, and 73.

20. George Oldendorp quoted in Brown, *Reaper's Garden*, 65.

21. Barbara Walker, *Out of the Ordinary: Folklore and the Supernatural* (Logan: Utah State University Press, 1995), 4.

22. Brown, *Reaper's Garden*, 5.

23. Laura Lomas, "Mystifying Mystery: Inscriptions of the Oral in the Legend of Rose Hall," *Journal of West Indian Literature* 6, no. 2 (1994): 70–87.

24. "Tragedy at Kendal—1957," *Jamaica Gleaner*, September 3, 2001.

25. "Hundreds Seek the Coffin and Crows," *Kingston Daily Gleaner*, Oct. 29, 1970, 1, 7.

26. "Tragedy at Kendal—1957"; all details of the crash come from this source.

27. Barbara Ellington, "Beverley East in Search of Answers—Book on Kendal Train Crash Coming," *Jamaica Gleaner*, September 29, 2002,

28. Paula Chen See, telephone conversation with author, Aug. 3, 2015.

29. Beverly East, *Reaper of Souls: A Novel of the 1957 Kendal Crash* (Kingston, Jamaica: Great House, 2007), 45.

30. Ibid., 111; subsequent quotations from and references to East in this paragraph come from pages 111 and 113–14.

31. "Tragedy at Kendal—1957."

32. "Death List," *Kingston Daily Gleaner*, Sept. 6, 1957.

33. Brown, *Reaper's Garden*, 204, 65.

34. George Simpson, "The Nine Night Ceremony in Jamaica," *Journal of American Folklore* 70, no. 278 (1957): 329–35.

35. "'Growing Disquiet Hits at Excursion 'Hooliganism,'" *Kingston Daily Gleaner*, Sept. 7, 1957.

36. "Hundreds Seek the Coffin and Crows."

37. Ibid.; all details of the incident come from this source.

38. Azizi Powell, "Caribbean Song 'One Solja Man,'" *Pancocojams* (blog), July 22, 2012, updated July 17, 2014, http://pancocojams.blogspot.com/2012/07/caribbean-song-one-solja-man.html.

39. *Encyclopedia Britannica* online, s.v. "turkey vulture."

40. Bob Marley and the Wailers, "Mr. Brown" (1970), track 3 on disc 2 of *Grooving Kingston 12* (box set), Hip-O Records, 2004.

41. "Who Is Mr. Brown?" *Kingston Daily Gleaner*, May 26, 2011.

42. Henry Hesketh Bell, *Obeah: Witchcraft in the West Indies*, 2nd ed. (London: Sampson Low, Marston, 1893), 46.

43. Martha Warren Beckwith, *Black Roadways: A Study of Jamaican Folk Life* (Chapel Hill: University of North Carolina Press, 1929), 76.

44. Brown, *Reaper's Garden*, 66; the subsequent quotation from Brown in this paragraph is also from 66.

45. James M. Phillippo, "Heathen Practices at Funerals" (engraving), in *Jamaica: Its Past and Present State*" (London: Snow, 1843), reproduced in Brown, *Reaper's Garden*, 67.

46. Brown, *Reaper's Garden*, 68.

47. Frederic Gomes Cassidy and Robert Brock Le Page, eds., *Dictionary of Jamaican English*, 2nd ed. (Kingston: University of the West Indies Press, 2002). Although "John Crow" and the term "Jim Crow" seem likely to have the same origin, according to the *Dictionary of Jamaican English*, the first recorded use of "John Crow" was in 1826 (250). According to the website of the Jim Crow Museum of Racist Memorabilia (at Ferris State University, Big Rapids, Michigan), the term "Jim Crow is often used to describe the segregation laws, rules, and customs which arose after Reconstruction ended in 1877 and continued until the mid-1960s" (https://www.ferris.edu/news/jimcrow/who). It was first used in 1828 as the stage name of a white actor who performed in blackface.

48. Cassidy and Le Page, *Dictionary of Jamaican English*, 251.

49. Powell, "Caribbean Song."

50. Anna Perkins Kasafi, "Of John Crows, Racial Ideology, and Contemporary Jamaica," Black History Month Lecture, 2014, *Jamaica Theological Seminary*, Feb. 18, 2014, http://home.jts.edu.jm/index.php/jts-blogs/182-black-history-month-lecture-2014.

51. Adewale Owoseni and Isaac Olufemi Olatoye, "Yoruba Ethico-Cultural Perspectives and Understanding of Animal Ethics," *Journal for Critical Animal Studies* 12, no.

3 (2014), criticalanimalstudies.org/wp-content/uploads/2014/08/JCAS-Vol-12-Issue-3-2014_2_FINAL.pdf; the quoted material from this article is from page 110.

52. John Rashford, "Plants, Spirits, and the Meaning of 'John' in Jamaica," *Jamaica Journal* 17, no. 2 (May 1984): 62; subsequent quotations from Bashford in this paragraph are from pages 62 and 65.

53. Beckwith, *Black Roadways*, 86.

54. Perkins, "Of John Crows."

55. Anthony Payne, *Rodney Riots in Jamaica: The Background and Significance of the Events of October 1968* (Cambridge: Cambridge University Press, 1983), 162; subsequent quotations from and references to Payne in this paragraph come from pages 159, 163, and 158.

56. Junie Ranks, "Shirley Duppy," video posted to YouTube by Ah Toms, Dec. 21, 2018, https://www.youtube.com/watch?v=bpEJbDXTE2o.

57. Ibid.

58. The DVD jacket lists only the name of the film, but no distributor or year of production (though some scenes in the film list the year 2002 from the camcorder). The short list of credits includes actors, hair and makeup support, and a lengthy number of executive producers: Kathlene Green, Yaynor Greenaway, Debbian Phenix, Delroy Beaumont, Maureen Jackson, and Felina Bailey.

59. Abbie Bakan, "How the IMF Wrecked Jamaica," *Socialist Worker*, July 10, 2007, https://socialistworker.co.uk/art/12087/How+the+IMF+wrecked+Jamaica.

60. Goldstein, Grider, and Thomas, *Haunting Experiences*, 39, 41.

61. Beckwith, *Black Roadways*, 75.

62. Brown, *Reaper's Garden*, 69.

63. Leonard E. Barrett, *The Sun and the Drum: African Roots in Jamaican Folk Tradition* (Portsmouth, N.H.: Heinemann, 1976), 108.

64. Beckwith, *Black Roadways*, 88.

65. "Caribbean Islands Foreign Assistance," *Encyclopedia of the Nations*, accessed Apr. 13, 2010, country-data.com/cgi-bin/query/r-3182.html.

66. Brown, *Reaper's Garden*, 68.

67. Goldstein, Grider, and Thomas, *Haunting Experiences*, 2.

CHAPTER FOUR. Exodus

Epigraph: Junot Díaz, *The Brief Wondrous Life of Oscar Wao* (London: Penguin, 2008), 6.

1. Brian W. Aldiss, *Billion Year Spree: The True History of Science Fiction* (New York: Doubleday, 1973), 20–31. For a contrasting view, see Patrick Brantlinger, "The Gothic Origins of Science Fiction," *Novel* 14, no. 1 (Autumn 1980): 30–43.

2. Maxwell Philip, *Emmanuel Appadocca; or, Blighted Life: A Tale of the Boucaneers*, ed. Reginald Cudjoe Selwyn and E. Cain William (London: Skeet, 1854; Amherst: University of Massachusetts Press, 1997); citations are to the University of Massachusetts Press edition. Thanks to my friend Faith Smith for the reference to *Emmanuel Appadocca*.

3. Ibid., 18; the subsequent quotation from the novel comes from page 36.

4. Darko Suvin, "On the Poetics of the Science Fiction Genre," *College English* 34, no. 3 (Dec. 1972): 375.

5. Christopher Columbus, "Letter from Columbus to Luis de Santangel," Feb. 15, 1493, 268, American Journeys Collection, document AJ-063, Wisconsin Historical Society Digital Library and Archives, 2003, americanjourneys.org/aj-063/index.asp; Alejo Carpentier, "On the Marvelous Real in America" (1949), in *Magical Realism: Theory, History, Community*, ed. Lois Parkinson Zamora and Wendy B. Faris (Durham, N.C.: Duke University Press, 1995), 88.

6. Mark Dery, "Black to the Future: Interviews with Samuel R. Delany, Greg Tate, and Tricia Rose," in *Flame Wars: The Discourse of Cyberculture*, ed. Mark Dery (Durham, N.C.: Duke University Press, 1994), 180.

7. Olaudah Equiano, *The Interesting Narrative of the Life of Olaudah Equiano*, ed. Robert J. Allison (1789; Boston: Bedford, 1995), 1; citations are to the Bedford edition. Subsequent references to and quotations from Equiano come from pages 3–4, 5, 47, and 53–54.

8. Kodwo Eshun, "Further Considerations of Afrofuturism," *New Centennial Review* 3, no. 2 (2003): 288.

9. Nalo Hopkinson and Uppinder Mehan, eds., *So Long Been Dreaming: Postcolonial Science Fiction and Fantasy* (Vancouver: Arsenal, 2010), ii–iii.

10. Elisabeth Anne Leonard, "Race and Ethnicity in Science Fiction," in *The Cambridge Companion to Science Fiction*, ed. Edward James and Farah Mendelsohn (Cambridge: Cambridge University Press, 2003), 254.

11. Thulani Davis quoted in De Witt Kilgore, *Astrofuturism* (Philadelphia: University of Pennsylvania Press, 2003), 18–19.

12. Kilgore, *Astrofuturism*, 16, 17.

13. Istvan Csicsery-Ronay Jr., *The Seven Beauties of Science Fiction* (Middletown, Conn.: Wesleyan University Press, 2008), 231.

14. John Rieder, "Embracing the Alien: Science Fiction in Mass Culture," *Science Fiction Studies* 9, no. 1 (Mar. 1982): 3.

15. Isiah Lavender, *Race in American Science Fiction* (Bloomington: Indiana University Press, 2011), 20.

16. Eric D. Smith, *Globalization, Utopia, and Postcolonial Science Fiction: New Maps of Hope* (New York: Palgrave Macmillan, 2012), 17.

17. Dery, "Black to the Future," 180.

18. Eshun, "Further Considerations of Afrofuturism," 290.

19. Tobias Buckell, "Stories of What-If," interview by Philip Sander, *Caribbean Beat*, March–April 2016, https://www.caribbean-beat.com/issue-138/stories-of-what-if #axzz5eDxAXHmd.

20. Derek Walcott, "The Sea is History," in *The Poetry of Derek Walcott, 1948–2013*, ed. Glyn Maxwell (New York: Farrar, Straus and Giroux, 2014), 253–56.

21. Lisa Yaszek, "Afrofuturism, Science Fiction, and the History of the Future," *Socialism and Democracy* 20, no. 3 (2006): 47.

22. Yaszek quite intriguingly argues that musical artists, including the Jamaican Lee "Scratch" Perry, fashioned "themselves (and by extension all Afrodiasporic people) as the descendants of aliens who came to Earth to prepare humanity for its eventual destiny among the stars" ("Afrofuturism," 46).

23. Buckell, "Stories of What-If."

24. Tobias S. Buckell, *Crystal Rain* (New York: Doherty, 2006), 47.

25. Smith, *Globalization, Utopia*, 189.

26. Buckell, *Crystal Rain*, 76; subsequent quotations in this paragraph come from pages 76 and 47.

27. Ibid., 49.

28. Ibid., 348.

29. Ibid.

30. Sharon DeGraw, "Tobias S. Buckell's Galactic Caribbean Future," *Extrapolation* 56, no. 1 (2015): 49.

31. Buckell, *Crystal Rain*, 115; subsequent references to and quotations from the novel are from pages 29, 98, and 115.

32. DeGraw, "Buckell's Galactic Caribbean Future," 47.

33. Buckell, *Crystal Rain*, 309.

34. Book jacket for Tobias S. Buckell, *Ragamuffin* (New York: Doherty, 2007).

35. "Grounation, aka Groundation, Day," Read the Spirit, https://www.readthespirit .com/religious-holidays-festivals/groundation-day-rastafarian-holiday-and-haile -selassie. This day is also notable as the day of the issuing of the dictum "liberation before repatriation."

36. DeGraw, "Buckell's Galactic Caribbean Future," 44.

37. Buckell, *Ragamuffin*, 94.

38. Ibid., 95.

39. Buckell, *Ragamuffin*, 102.

40. DeGraw, "Buckell's Galactic Caribbean Future," 53–54.

41. Tobias Buckell, *Sly Mongoose* (New York: Doherty, 2008), 11, book jacket.

42. Ibid., 14; subsequent references to the novel in this paragraph come from pages 12, 18, and 13.

43. Ibid., 31.

44. Homer, *The Odyssey of Homer*, trans. Richmond Lattimore (New York: Harper & Row, 1965), 117, 118.

45. Ibid., 23; other references to and quotations from the novel in this paragraph are from pages 24–25 and 28–29.

46. Ibid., 27; other references to the novel are from page 26.

47. Ibid., 38; other references to and quotations from the novel in this paragraph are from pages 34, 38, and 31.

48. Ibid., 32.

49. Buckell, "Stories of What-If"; DeGraw, "Buckell's Galactic Caribbean Future," 48.

50. DeGraw, "Buckell's Galactic Caribbean Future," 41.

51. Hopkinson, *So Long Been Dreaming*, ii–iii.

52. Fredric Jameson, *Archaeologies of the Future: The Desire Called Utopia, and Other Science Fictions* (New York: Verso, 2005), 286.

53. Derek Walcott, "The Caribbean: Culture or Mimicry?," *Journal of InterAmerican Studies and World Affairs* 16, no. 1 (1974): 6.

54. Chimamanda Ngozi Adichie, "The Danger of a Single Story," TED, July 2009, timestamp 18:49, https://www.ted.com/talks/chimamanda_adichie_the_danger_of_a_single_story?language=en.

55. Walter Mosley, "Black to the Future," in *Dark Matter: A Century of Speculative Future from the African Diaspora*, ed. Sheree Thomas (New York: Warner, 2000), 202–3.

CONCLUSION. Seeing Strange Things

Epigraph: Christopher Columbus, "Letter from Columbus to Luis de Santangel," Feb. 15, 1493, 268, American Journeys Collection, document AJ-063, Wisconsin Historical Society Digital Library and Archives, 2003, americanjourneys.org/aj-063/index.asp.

1. For the Brian Wong Won series known as the "dancing houses" (1995–2012), see the website of Brian Wong Won: Fine Art & Design, https://brianwongwon.wixsite.com/bww-artdesign/architecture.

2. Edward J. Sullivan, *Continental Shifts: The Art of Edouard Duval Carrié* (Miami: American Art Corporation, 2007), 5.

3. April Ann Shemak, *Asylum Speakers: Caribbean Refugees and Testimonial Discourse* (New York: Fordham University Press, 2011), 129.

4. See Erica Moiah James's discussion of Duval-Carrié's *Mardi Gras at Fort Diman-*

che: Erica Moiah James, "Speaking in Tongues: Metapictures and the Discourse of Violence in Caribbean Art," Small Axe 16, no. 1 (2012): 119–43.

5. Duval-Carrié to the author, email, May 16, 2017.

6. Ibid.

7. Alejo Carpentier, *The Kingdom of This World*, trans. Harriet De Onís (1949; Eng. trans., 1957; New York: Macmillan, 2006), 89. Citations refer to the Macmillan edition.

8. For Asser Saint-Val's biography, see his website, https://www.assersaintvl.com.

9. Asser Saint-Val, interview by the author, May 10, 2018, Miami Beach, Florida.

10. Saint-Val's website, https://www.assersaintvl.com.

11. Merriam Webster online, s.v. "surrealism."

12. André Breton, *Manifestoes of Surrealism*, trans. Richard Seaver and Helen R. Lane (Ann Arbor: University of Michigan Press, 1969), 10.

APPENDIX. Interview with Tobias Buckell

1. Darko Suvin, "On the Poetics of the Science Fiction Genre," *College English* 34, no. 3 (Dec. 1972): 375.

2. Mark Dery, ed., *Flame Wars: The Discourse of Cyberculture* (Durham, N.C.: Duke University Press, 1994), 180.

3. Nalo Hopkinson, *So Long Been Dreaming: Postcolonial Science Fiction and Fantasy* (Vancouver: Arsenal, 2010), ii–iii.

4. Elizabeth M. Ginway, "A Working Model for Analyzing Third World Science Fiction: The Case of Brazil," *Science Fiction Studies* 32, no. 3 (Nov. 2005): 467.

INDEX

abjection, 44
Abolition of Slavery Act (1833), 38
Act to Remedy the Evils Arising from Irregular Assemblies of Slaves (1760), 36
African Americans, 60, 74–75, 103, 122, 138–39
African diaspora, 3, 11, 67, 91; black leadership and, 74; Buckell's novels and, 113, 114; death discourses and, 81–82; science fiction and, 25, 102–5, 123, 139; vampirism and, 5
Afrofuturism, 25, 122; Buckell's thoughts on, 138–40; definition, 106
agency, 2–3, 12, 93; of the disembodied, 89, 99; zombie's lack of, 62, 63
Ajanaku, Femi, 74
Aldiss, Brian W., 100
alienation, 46, 104, 121, 140
aliens, 68–69, 110, 113, 142, 160n22
American Horror Story (TV series), 12, 133
Anatol, Giselle, 4–5
Aravamudan, Srinivas, 34–35
audiences, 28, 48, 58, 65, 66

Babylon, 108
Bad Boys II (2003), 43, 66, 70–71, 73, 74
Bakan, Abbie, 98
Baker, Josephine, 56
Barrett, Leonard, 98

Bassett, Sally, 79
Baucom, Ian, 81
Beckwith, Martha, 93, 95, 98
Bell, Hesketh, 92–93
Bell, Sir Henry, 153n36
Bellin, Joshua, 46–47, 77
Bennett, Gillian, 81
Bermuda, 79, 146n22
Bilby, Kenneth, 4, 15, 26–27
blackness, 27–28, 120; dreadlocks and, 50, 51, 69; dystopia and, 106; experience of, 131, 132; monstrosity and, 74–75; pathologizing, 30, 63, 68–70; physiological, 15; sci-fi and, 104–5; zombie films and, 60
Black Pirate, The (1926), 51
black power movements, 73–74
body, 33, 103; black female, 56–57, 58; black male, 70, 74; Caribbean, 77; limbs, 130, 131–32; of the monster, 65; white female, 62–63
boloms, 14, 79
Bolster, W. Jeffrey, 51, 153n31
Boukman, Dutty, 12, 29, 146n22
Boyce, William, 7
Braham, Persephone, 46
Breton, André, 133
Bride of Frankenstein (1935), 65

163

Britain: abolition of slavery, 38; black sovereignty in, 40–41; relations with Jamaica, 13, 89–90

British literature: Obeah discussions, 26–28, 32–35; portrayal of "natives," 31–32; sociohistorical context, 37–41

Brown, Vincent, 82–83, 89, 93, 98, 99

Browne, Randy, 36

Buckell, Tobias, 2, 101, 106; author interview with, 121–22, 135–43; on the Caribbean experience, 107; *Crystal Rain*, 108–13, 142; *Ragamuffin*, 113–15; *Sly Mongoose*, 115–19, 142; "Toy Planes," 142; Xenowealth series discussion, 2–3, 14, 107–8, 119–21

Calypso, 55–57

cannibalism, 7–8, 29, 145n9

Caribbean: deployments of the fantastic, 1–4, 12, 44; history and memory, 38, 39, 54, 107, 111, 113, 122–23, 139; Hollywood's influence, 42, 47–49; infusion of magic, 72, 77; literary writers, 14, 24, 100–102, 136; as monstrous, 63–64, 66, 74–75; murder rate, 77; populous nations, 13; scholarly studies, 4–6, 41

carnival space, 125–26

Carpentier, Alejo: *The Kingdom of This World*, 11–12, 21–22, 127–28; "On the Marvelous Real in America," 103

Caruth, Cathy, 81

Cassuto, Leonard, 44

Chamoiseau, Patrick, 14, 101

Christianity, 7, 9, 15, 18, 19, 33, 89

citizenship, 75, 121

Clarke, Sebastian, 51

colonialism, 13, 36, 77; Buckell's retelling of, 112, 114, 115, 119, 121, 122–23; the Caribbean fantastic and, 2, 3, 5; fantastical cinema and, 43, 44–46; ghost narratives and, 81, 99; power and dominance of, 30, 31; sci-fi and, 105; superiority claims, 32, 58

colonial literature. *See* British literature

Columbus, Christopher, 125

community memory, 99

Consuming the Caribbean: From Arawaks to Zombies (Sheller), 5–6

consumption trope, 5–6

Cops, 70

counterculture, 50–52

Creed, Barbara, 57

crime thrillers, 24, 43; Afro-Caribbean spiritual practices in, 66–68, 70–71, 73; black political leadership in, 72, 74; portrayal of blackness in, 68–70, 74–75. *See also specific titles*

criminal activity, 28, 33, 74; immigrants and, 67, 75–76; in Jamaica, 76–77, 89–90, 96. *See also* drug trade; lawlessness

crows. *See* John crows

Csicsery-Ronay, Istvan, 45, 105

Cuba, 12, 13, 70, 146n22

cultural myths, 141–42

curses, 9, 33

cyborgs, 2, 68, 113, 114, 118

Dash, Michael, 7, 8

Davies, Owen, 16–17

Davis, Thulani, 104

Davis, Wade, 66

Dayan, Joan (Colin), 5, 8, 44, 62

death discourses, 81–84; significance of crows, 91, 95. *See also* funerary rituals

debts and debtors, 8, 77, 93, 96–99

Dégh, Linda, 79–80, 81, 83

DeGraw, Sharon, 112, 113, 114, 115, 119

Dekker, Desmond, 48–49

de Laurence, Lauron William, 16–19

democracy, 118

Dendle, Peter, 59–60, 65

Depp, Johnny, 43, 49–50, 52

Derrida, Jacques, 6

Dery, Mark, 103, 106, 138

Deslippe, Philip, 18

developing countries, 117, 119

INDEX

Díaz, Junot, 100
disembodiment, 78, 82, 88, 89, 99, 132
disempowerment, 46–47
Disney, 49, 50, 55, 58
"Does God Hate Haiti?" (Mohler), 10
dreadlocks, 114; of gangster monsters, 68–69, 71, 73–74; worn in *Pirates of the Caribbean*, 50, 51, 52, 53, 55, 152n26
Dred Scott v. Sandford, 75
drug trade, 67–68, 70, 71, 73, 76, 115; Rastafarianism and, 74. *See also* criminal activity
duppy stories. *See* ghost stories
Duval-Carrié, Edouard, 126–30, 133

Edwards, Bryan, 27–29, 31–33, 38–39, 40
Eisner, Michael, 50
Ellington, Barbara, 86
Emmanuel Appadocca; or, Blighted Life: A Tale of the Boucaneers (Philip), 100–101
Emperor Jones, The (1933), 72–73
English in the West Indies, The (Froude), 27–29, 32, 38, 40–41
enslaved people. *See* slavery
Equiano, Olaudah, 103–4, 113, 123
Eshun, Kodwo, 104, 106
Exceptional Violence (Thomas), 76, 77
exotic, constructs of, 18–19
Eҳili Intercepted (Duval-Carrié), 127

fantastic, term usage, 20–21
fantasy film, 45–46, 152n15
folklore, 79–80, 114, 155n6
Forde, Maarit, 31
France, 13, 36
Frank, Kevin, 55, 152n26
Frankenstein (Shelley), 100
Froude, James Anthony, 27–29, 32, 38, 40–41
Fuentes, Yvette, 146n22
funerary rituals, 33, 83, 84, 98, 99; coffins and bearers, 92–93; nine-night ceremony, 89. *See also* death discourses

gangsters: Jamaican, 35, 76; monsters, 43, 66–71, 73–74, 77
Garvey, Marcus, 3, 113
gaze, the, 42, 44, 65, 66
ghosts, 24, 78; Derrida on, 6; different names for, 79; in films, 54, 72; spirits of the deceased, 89; tourism, 49, 84; in visual art, 125. *See also* paranormal
ghost stories: in Caribbean context, 78–79; cultural beliefs and, 80; Duppy Shirley story, 85, 96–99; hauntings in Jamaica, 22, 24, 78, 84–85; Kendal train crash, 85–90; theoretical approaches to, 79–81
Gikandi, Simon, 26, 38–39, 41
Ginway, M. Elizabeth, 141
Girard, René, 46–47
Goveia, Elsa, 37–38, 40, 41
grotesqueness, 44, 57, 66
Guerrero, Ed, 45, 47
Gunst, Laurie, 76–77

Haiti: Carpentier's visit to, 11–12, 22; earthquake (2010), 9–10; independence, 29; Jamaica connection, 12; population, 13; slave revolts, 29, 66; "strangeness" construction, 7–9; visual art, 126–27. *See also* Vodun
Haitian Revolution, 13, 22, 128, 146n22; U.S. role, 6–7, 66; Vodun and, 9–11
Hall, Stuart, 42
Hammond, Dorothy, 30
Handler, Jerome, 4, 26–27
Harder They Come, The (1972), 35, 48
Harris, Naomie, 55
Harris, Wilson, 41, 78
Hartman, Saidiya, 81
Haunting Experiences (Thomas), 98, 99
hauntings. *See* ghosts; ghost stories
healers, 37
Henry, Paget, 31
higglers, 114–15
Hinduism, 18

History, Civil and Commercial, of the British Colonies in the West Indies, The (Edwards): critique, 27, 38–39; historical methodology, 40; narrative style, 28; Obeah constructs, 28–29, 33, 35

History of Jamaica, The (Long): Afro-Caribbean belief systems, 2, 3–4; approach to historiography, 40; narrative style, 28; Obeah practitioners, 2, 22, 28, 32, 33–34; sociohistorical context, 27, 37, 38

Hollywood, 42, 43, 51, 55, 60, 77; anxieties about miscegenation, 65; dreadlocks and, 50, 152n26; influence on Caribbean culture, 47–49

home: Buckell's idea of, 121, 136; yearning for, 112, 114, 115

hooks, bell, 56

Hopkinson, Nalo, 14, 101, 102, 106, 121; *So Long Been Dreaming: Postcolonial Science Fiction and Fantasy*, 104, 140

hypnotism, 16, 17

identity: African, 74; American immigrant, 75; blackness, 51, 52, 69–70; Caribbean, 3, 44, 49, 55, 65, 73; cultural, 83; of literary/movie characters, 48; monstrous, 46, 57–58, 64, 77; Obeah and Vodun, 6; subaltern, 127

immigrants: Buckell's experience, 121, 137; lawlessness and, 67, 75–76; racial identity and, 75; sending remittances, 97; zombies as, 59

immortality, 83

International Monetary Fund (IMF), 76, 97–98, 99, 117

In the Wake of Columbus (Ober), 7

I Walked with a Zombie (1943), 8, 43, 60, 62, 63–65

Iwasaka, Michiko, 80

Jablow, Alta, 30

Jamaica, 6, 15, 16, 29, 34, 40; ban on publications, 1, 17; Haiti connection, 12; hauntings in, 14, 22, 24, 84–85; IMF borrowing, 97–98, 99; income and unemployment, 77, 95, 98; independence from Britain, 89–90; population, 13; rebellions and riots, 13, 95–96; sayings, 91, 92; violence, 51–52, 76–77; working class, 92, 93

James, C. L. R., 11

James Bond. See *Live and Let Die* (1973)

Jameson, Frederic, 122

JanMohamed, Abdul, 31–32

Jim Crow laws, 65, 75, 157n47

John crows, 90–95, 99, 157n47

Journal of a West India Proprietor (Lewis), 23, 27–29, 32–33, 35, 38

juju, term usage, 1

Kee, Chera, 65–66

Kendal train crash (1957), 85–90

Kilgore, De Witt, 105

Kingdom of this World, The (Carpentier), 11–12, 21–22; Duval-Carrié's drawing, 127–29; plot, 128

King of the Zombies (1941), 8, 43, 60–61, 63–64

Kordas, Ann, 59

Kristeva, Julia, 44

Kuumba, M., 74

La Grotte des poisons (Duval-Carrié), 129–30

"La Luz de Yara," 146n22

La Main Broyé (Duval-Carrié), 129

Latin American literature, 21–23

Lauro, Sarah, 8, 59

Lavender, Isiah, III, 45, 47, 105, 123, 152n16

Lawless, Robert, 7

lawlessness, 35, 50, 75–76, 89. See also criminal activity

legend, definition, 79–80

Leonard, Elizabeth, 104

Lévi-Strauss, Claude, 88

Lewis, Matthew "Monk," 23, 27–29, 32–33, 35, 38

Lim, Bliss Cua, 45
Live and Let Die (1973), 43, 66–68, 71–72, 74
living dead, 82–83
loans, 97–98, 99
Lomas, Laura, 84
Long, Edward: *The History of Jamaica*, 2–4, 22, 27–29, 31–34; sociohistorical context of works, 37, 38, 40
Lord, Karen, 14, 101, 106, 138

MacDonald, William, 80
Mackie, Erin, 51
magic: books, 16–17; of carnival space, 125; in *The Emperor Jones* (1933), 72; gangster monsters and, 66, 67, 70, 71–73; high-tech, 18; oppressive, 5, 44; potion, 64; slave rebellions and, 37; song references, 14–15
magical realism, 21–23, 128
Magic Island, The (Seabrook), 8–9
Makandal (*houngan*), 12, 29, 127–30
Mansong, Jack, 34–35
marginalization, 44, 46, 51, 72, 121; racial, 119–20
Marked for Death (1990), 43, 66–68, 70, 71, 74
Marley, Bob, 50, 74, 96; "Mr. Brown," 92, 93
Maroons, 51, 54; Nanny heroine of, 1, 4, 79, 146n22; wars, 13
Mastiffs Cubain (Duval-Carrié), 128
Mbembe, Achille, 82
Mbiti, John, 82–83
McClintock, Anne, 45
McIntosh, Shawn, 60
Mda, Zakes, 23
mediums, 93
melanin, 131–32
Miguel Street (Naipul), 48
Mintz, Sidney, 43, 51
miscegenation, 65
modernity, 38, 39, 80, 104; Afro-Caribbean spirituality and, 3, 20, 31
Mohler, R. Albert, Jr., 10, 11
mongoose, 120

monsters: camera framing of, 23–24, 46, 55; dogs as, 128; gangster, 43, 66–71, 73–74; identity, 57–58, 77; metaphors of the Caribbean, 46–47, 63–64, 66. *See also* zombie films; zombies
Morrison, Toni, 104
mortuary politics, 82, 83
Moseley, Benjamin, 34–35
Mosley, Walter, 123
movement and mobility, 15, 113, 114, 119, 131–32
"Mr. Brown" (Marley), 92, 93
Munro, Martin, 78–79
Myalism, 4, 29, 39
myths, evolution of, 88, 146n22

Nama, Adilifu, 45, 69
Nanny (Maroon leader), 1, 4, 79, 146n22
National Geographic, 7
New York City, 37

Obeah, 1, 2, 4, 17, 97; in British literature, 26–30, 32–35; conflated with Vodun, 6, 73; European anxieties about, 13, 35–36, 38, 39, 40; healers, 37; outlawing of, 36; planters and, 39; science tradition and, 13, 19–20; slave uprisings and, 29–30; songs referencing, 3, 15–16; Tia Dalma character as, 12, 52, 53, 55
"Obeah Wedding" (Mighty Sparrow), 3, 15
Obi; or, The History of Three-Fingered Jack (Earle), 34–35, 133
Ocean's 11 (1960), 49
Odyssey (Homer), 55–56, 116
"Oil, The" (Lovindeer), 15–16
One Love Peace Concert (1978), 51–52, 76
"007 Shanty Town" (Dekker), 49
oppression, 30, 77, 108, 112, 120, 146n22; alien, 113, 120; Buckell's thoughts on, 139–40, 142–43
Other/Otherness, 18–19, 30–31, 32, 43, 45
outlaws, 35, 51–52, 57, 66

pallbearers, 92–93, 98
Palmer, Annie, 84
paranormal, 16, 79; belief in, 80; definition, 20. *See also* ghosts; ghost stories
Paton, Diana, 31, 35, 40, 41; Obeah commentary, 13, 28, 38, 39
Payne, Anthony, 95–96
Perkins, Anna Kasafi, 94, 95
Perry, Lee "Scratch," 160n22
Peterson, Ann, 50
Peter the Doctor (rebellion leader), 37
Phillippo, James, 93
pirates, 43, 153n31; films, 24, 50; rude boys as contemporary, 51–52; sci-fi novels, 100–101
Pirates of the Caribbean series: gross earnings, 49; Jack Sparrow character, 43, 49–50, 52, 152n26; portrayal of the Caribbean, 152n15; Tia Dalma character, 12, 44, 52–58, 77
plantations, 38, 62, 84; Long's account of, 2, 4, 22
plantocracy, 12, 13, 36, 39, 41
poisonings, 33–34, 36, 128
political leadership, 72, 74
Polk, Patrick, 17, 19
popular culture, 12, 43, 59, 66
power dynamics, 137–38
Predator (1987), 66, 69–70
Predator II (1990), 43, 66, 68–69, 71, 74
primitivism, 8, 11, 30, 36
psychics, 71, 73; Miss Cleo, 1, 55
Putnam, Lara, 41

race and racialization: colonial power and, 30; fantasy and, 45–46; immigration and, 75–76; John crows and, 93–94; portrayals in film, 43, 47, 60, 65, 68–70; sci-fi and, 45, 104–5, 119–20, 123; skin pigmentation, 131; stereotypes, 56–57
racial difference, 31, 32, 34, 105
radical irrationalism, 26, 39
Ragamuffin, term usage, 120
Rashford, John, 95

Rastafarianism, 17, 50, 73–74, 95; "grounation" day, 114, 160n35
Reaper of Souls (East), 87–88
Reckord, Mary, 13
Reeder, James, 35
reggae, 48, 50, 70, 92, 96, 138. *See also* Marley, Bob
religious practices. *See* spiritual practices
revenge, 98, 127
Richardson, Michael, 43
Rieder, John, 45, 47, 105, 123
Robertson, Pat, 9–10, 11
Rodney, Walter, 96
Roh, Franz, 21
Romero, George, 59
Rose Hall Great House (Jamaica), 49, 84
Rucker, Walter, 29, 35, 37
rude boys, 49, 50, 51–52, 57

sacrifices: animal, 9, 70, 95; human, 29, 111
Said, Edward, 58
Saint-Val, Asser, 22, 130–33
Samuel, Kameelah, 54, 55, 58
Santeria, 12, 70
Savage, John, 36
savagery, 129; Obeah practices and, 27, 33, 39; Western literary constructions, 30–31
"savage slot," 30–31
scapegoating, 46, 47, 60
Schmidt, Hans, 11, 146n13
science fiction: African diaspora and, 25, 102–5, 123; in Brazil, 141; Buckell's comments on, 121–22, 123, 137–40; Caribbean writers, 14, 101–2; definition of genre, 102, 137; first novels written, 100–101; futuristic concerns, 106; Jameson on, 122; race and, 104–5; steampunk, 109. *See also* Afrofuturism; Buckell, Tobias
science tradition, 13, 14–16, 19
Seabrook, William, 8–9
self-governance/self-determination, 4, 11, 29, 113, 139

sexuality, 94; black women's, 56–57; of women in zombie films, 62–63
Sharp, Granville, 38
Sheller, Mimi, 5–6, 145n9
Shemak, April, 127
Shirley Duppy (film), 97, 158n58
"Shirley Duppy" (song), 97
"skankin," meaning, 92
skin pigment, 131–32
slavery, 7, 82, 99, 142; alien-abduction tale and, 25, 102–4; Buckell's retelling of, 108, 112–13, 115, 119, 121, 122–23; funerary rituals, 83; horrors and trauma of, 37, 54, 129–30, 133, 140; portrayals in film, 12, 54, 65, 140; pro-slavery arguments, 40, 41; punishments, 5, 45; racialization and, 43, 94; rebellions and Obeah, 13, 27, 29–30, 33–37, 38; U.S. Revolution and, 140
slave trade, 38, 39, 81, 108, 113, 156n14
Smith, Eric, 109
Smith, Faith, 40–41
sovereignty, 11, 30, 38; in British colonies, 40–41; Buckell's retelling of, 112–13, 115; Caribbean, 107, 122, 123, 146n22; death and, 82
speculative fiction genre, 20
spirit child, 81
spiritual practices: in Buckell's novels, 111–12, 142; death beliefs and practices, 82–83, 89; de Laurence's influence on, 16–19; European anxieties about, 35–36, 39; of gangster monsters, 65, 70–71, 73; inflected in visual art, 125–27; Long's account, 2, 3–4; modernity and, 31, 39; oppression and, 142–43; rejection of, 35; scholarly studies on, 4; science tradition of, 14–15; slave uprisings and, 29, 34–35, 37. *See also* Christianity; Obeah; Vodun
St. John, Spenser, 41
St. Lucia, 14, 79
stage names, 48
steampunk, 109, 132

Sullivan, Edward, 126
supernatural, 5, 6, 9, 19, 26, 28; belief in, 34, 81; definition, 20; encounters, 24; gangster monsters and, 66, 68, 70, 71, 72. *See also* ghosts; ghost stories
surrealism, definition, 133
Suvin, Darko, 102, 137

technology, 103, 106, 113, 116, 118, 123; steampunk, 109, 132
Tehranian, John, 75
Things That Fly in the Night, The (Anatol), 4–5
Thomas, Deborah, 76, 77
Thomas, Jeannie, 80, 98, 99
Todorov, Tzvetan, 21, 23
Toelken, Barre, 80
Tosh, Peter, 51–52, 76
tourism, 49, 76, 84, 119, 142
trauma, 5, 65, 81, 111, 122; of slavery, 54, 103
travel writers, 30
tribal practices, 69, 72–73
Trinidad, 48
Trouillot, Michel-Rolph, 30–31

United States, 65, 76, 114; relationship with Haiti, 6–7, 8, 11, 66
Universal Negro Improvement Association (UNIA), 113

vampires, 5, 21
Van Duzer, Chet, 46
Vickerman, Milton, 152n15
violence, 46, 58, 126, 128, 129; in Jamaica, 51–52, 76–77, 95–96
visual artists, 21; Caribbean, 25, 125–33; European, 22
Vodun, 6, 58; Carpentier's observations, 11–12; Erzulie (loa), 52, 127; gangster monsters and, 67, 70–71, 73; ignorance of, 73; priest (*houngan*), 12, 29, 146n22; role in Haitian Revolution, 9–11; texts and studies, 4; and

Vodun (*continued*)
"voodoo" usage, 23; in zombie films, 8, 60, 61, 62, 64, 65–66
vultures, 94–95. *See also* John crows

Walcott, Derek, 101, 106, 123
Walker, Barbara, 81, 83
Warner, Keith, 48
western genre, 48
West Indies, 38, 40, 152n15
"Wheel and Turn Me" (song), 94
whiteness, 75, 94; hegemony, 106, 132
White Zombie (1932), 8, 43, 60, 61–64
Wilson-Tagoe, Nana, 39–41
witchcraft or sorcery, 15, 28–29, 58. *See also* Vodun
"Witch Doctor" (Mighty Sparrow), 16
women: black, 55, 56–57; white, 8, 60, 61–63, 65
Wong Won, Brian, 125–26, 133
World Bank, 76, 98, 99, 117
Wynter, Sylvia, 31

Xenowealth series (Buckell): *Crystal Rain*, 108–13, 142; overview and discussion, 107–8, 119–20, 122–24; *Ragamuffin*, 113–15; *Sly Mongoose*, 115–19, 142

Yanique, Tiphanie, 14, 102
Yaszek, Lisa, 106, 160n22
Yoruba, 94–95; divination practice, 53, 73
Yoss (José Miguel Sánchez Gómez), 101, 133
Young, Elizabeth, 65

zombie films: ancestral roots, 59, 66; colonialism/imperialism and, 24, 43; and constructions of the Caribbean, 63–65, 152n15; racial issues in, 60; Romero's, 59; white female fragility theme, 8, 61–63
zombies: in American popular culture, 59, 66; in Buckell's novels, 117, 119; zombification, 71
Zong (ship), 81

www.ingramcontent.com/pod-product-compliance
Lightning Source LLC
Chambersburg PA
CBHW030655230426
43665CB00011B/1109